Twenty Steps Toward a Climate of Justice

With 116 posts
from the
Climate of Justice Blog
2020 - 2024

Marvin T. Brown

authorHOUSE·

AuthorHouse™
1663 Liberty Drive
Bloomington, IN 47403
www.authorhouse.com
Phone: 833-262-8899

Published by AuthorHouse 01/30/2025

ISBN: 979-8-8230-4042-6 (sc)
ISBN: 979-8-8230-4041-9 (e)

Library of Congress Control Number: 2024927245

Print information available on the last page.

About the Book

This book provides a multilayered approach--twenty steps--on how we might move toward a social climate of justice. Posts written for the Climate of Justice Project exemplify how the steps direct us toward meaningful engagement with our social, political, and environmental challenges. The 116 posts were written as responses to conflicts, ideas, and conversations between 2020 and 2024.

Many of the posts are instances of dialogue with over 60 authors who have contributed to public discourse, such as Richard Powers, Roxanne Dunbar-Ortiz, and Robin Wall Kimmerer. Some posts are more philosophical than others, and some more humorous, such as the imaginary interview with Amy Coney Barrett.

The first step **Focus the Mind on a Climate of Justice** lays out the basic premise of the book, with eight posts including *Who will Protect us?* and *A Framework for our Thinking.* The second step **Take Care of Civic Spaces** defines the civic as the space where we can reconcile social differences and repair social damages. Step three addresses a common barrier to a climate of justice: authoritarian zealots, with four posts including *A Message to Christian Nationalism.*

The seventeen other steps, from **Abolish White Supremacy** to **Care for Civilians** include posts that respond to such events as Black Lives Matter, the coronavirus, the Russian invasion of Ukraine, and October 7. While the events keep changing, taking the steps that will move us toward a climate of justice have become even more relevant.

Marvin Brown's book Twenty Steps Toward a Climate of Justice offers a critical perspective on the challenges of this time of growing division among US citizens. His twenty steps reflect on the roots of how we got here and provide approaches we can take to come together. Taking a systemic approach to this important work, Marvin demonstrates the need to address the climate of injustice, which was created in the early days of this nation through acts of slavery and genocide and continues today in many forms. He argues that we cannot effectively address climate change until we work together to create a climate of justice. During this time, when fear of an uncertain future pushes our nation toward authoritarian leadership, Marvin's book offers hope through understanding, compassion, and coming together through civic action.

Nancy Southern
Saybrook University
Pasadena CA

For the past few years Marvin Brown's Climate of Justice has been just the ray of hope I've so desperately needed. Few have the courage to take on the issues of race, inequities and injustice and even fewer do it with Marvin's compassion, commitment, and understanding. Marvin is a true ally for those fighting for justice.

Donald Carter
Retired educator
Oakland, CA

As a long-time reader of Marvin Brown's blogpost, A Climate of Justice, I am gratified to see the publication of his new book *Twenty Steps Toward a Climate of Justice*. Each of the twenty steps called for are powerful, but in bringing them together as a model for one way we can move forward together their power is magnified several times over. Several of the steps call for a reckoning with our past and the ways in which we have created "American prosperity" by dominating and subduing both the earth and many of the earth's most vulnerable human inhabitants.

Brown's approach is that when we change the social climate from one in which conservative and authoritarian politics and corporate interests dominate to one in which the civic realm is much more prominent, we change the nature of our relationships, including those of citizen and civilian, to a focus on human dignity.

Twenty Steps Toward a Climate of Justice is a powerful book and offers a coherent vision for what we need most—a change in our images of self and of our social collective, such that recognition of our needs and responsibilities toward one another is pivotal. Only then, does our planet have a chance.

Arthur Jensen, Professor Emeritus
Department of Communication and Rhetorical Studies
Syracuse University

Contents

Introduction xv

Step 1. Focus the Mind on A Climate of Justice 1

Climate of Justice and Climate Justice 1
Who will protect us? 2
Living in a Climate of Injustice 4
The Resiliency of Evil 4
A Promise without a Soul 6
A Framework for Our Thinking 8
The Climate in Egypt and Qatar 9
Signs of Justice 10

Step 2. Take Care of Civic Spaces 13

Citizens and Civilians 13
The Civic and the Christian Imagination 14
Is America a Nation without a Country? 16
Civic vs Religious Disagreement 19
Cooperation vs Domination 20
The Civic Context of Political Campaigns 22
Our Political Climate is in Crisis 23
Time for a Civic Conscience 25

Step 3. Guard against Authoritarian Zealots 27

Trump's America 27
What Kind of Trouble Are We In? 29
Christian Zionism and American "Civil Religion" 30
A Message to Christian Nationalists 32
Who has been Chosen? 33

Step 4. Honor our Human Dignity 34

To be Born or Created 34
Putin's humanity 36
Human Dignity and Civic Spaces 37
Our Shared, but Not Common Humanity 39

Step 5. Protect the Earth 41

Why has the Environmental Movement failed us? 41
Earth Day 2020 and the Coronavirus 43
Protecting the Earth's Integrity 44
Why do we exist? 45

Step 6. Critically Value the Law 48

A Climate of Justice and the Rule of Law 48
My Interview with Amy Coney Barrett 49
The Rule of Law vs the Law of Rule 53
How can Catholics become Originalists? 54
The Sacred and the Solemn 55

Step 7. Care for Civilians 58

The Climate of Justice and the Protection of Civilians 58
Thinking like a Civilian 59
The Civilian's Condition 60
Jeremiah in Ukraine 63
Ukrainian Resistance and American Memories 64
Civilians after October 7 65

Step 8. Overcome National Amnesia 67

If Truth Be Told 67
America's Soul and The Climate of Injustice 68
The Trouble with Christian Nationalism 71
Considering "America" 73
The Principle of Coherence and Conflicting Memories 74
Our Domestic Imperial Climate 76
What's the Problem? 77

Step 9. Repair Social Damage..79

Are Reparations Necessary? 79
What to Replace and What to Repair..82
A Case for Reparations..83
Philanthropy vs Reparations 84
Reparations Benefit All of Us 86

Step 10. Change the Conversation 88

The Coronavirus and the Language of War................................88
It's not like war, it's like the New Deal 89
Trump Voters vs. Public Health..91
The Public and the Social 93
When is it a Mistake to Agree to Disagree? 94
Language matters: "Plantation" or "Slave Farm"? 95
D.E.I. vs U.M.E...97
Digital and Human Languages 98

Step 11. Highlight the Context...101

Why we need Contextual Thinking 101
Expanding our Contextual Awareness 103
The Context of Character 105
*A Conceivable Letter to People like House Representative
Mike Johnson*...107

Step 12. Interrupt Monocultural Thinking 109

The Clash of Stories on the National Mall...............................109
Critical White Theory..110
Whose History is Upon Us?..112
Telling Multiple Stories 116

Step 13. Abolish White Supremacy 118

Education for White People..118
White Men of Nebraska 119
The White Storm..121
The Abolition of the Master Class..122

Dealing with White Distortion 123

Writing While White 124

The White Dream of Safety 126

Step 14. Distribute Provisions Fairly 128

What part of corporations do you want to stimulate? 128

Farm Loyalty and Meat Processing Plants 129

Who Will Pay for This? 132

Prosperity and Justice 134

How To Protect What We Share 136

How Should We Share the Crop? 138

Let money and knowledge flow freely 140

Public Bias 142

Step 15. Change Course 144

Resetting our American Thermostat 144

The Pandemic and Climate Change 145

Better or Different 146

Will the Epidemic Change Social Habits? 147

They Knew. So What? 148

Choose your Past, Choose your Future 150

Step 16. Dissolve the Climate of Fear 151

The Coronavirus Exposure of Social Insecurity 151

What Happens When Fear Encounters Justice? 152

Dignity, and the Climate of Fear 153

Step 17. Acknowledge Limitations 156

Limiting American Prosperity 156

The American Tragedy 158

Biden's Mistake 159

Pie in the Sky, Mud in Your Eye 160

Listening to Reinhold Niebuhr 161

Step 18. Learn from Differences 162

Good Friday Reflections During the Epidemic 162

Afropessimism and White masters 164

Black Lives Matter and Thanks-taking 165

Critical Race Theory and Coherence 166

Joy in a Climate of Injustice 167

Step 19. Engage in Ethical Analysis 170

The Ethics of Biden's Withdrawal from Afghanistan. 170

An Ethical Foundation for Environmentalism 172

Three Images of Our Federal Government 175

Ethics of Politics 176

Ethics of the 14ᵗʰ Amendment 179

Step 20. Stand with Others for Social Justice 181

The Dangers of Compromise 181

71 Million and National Unity 183

Our Choice: Unity or Justice 184

The Voice of Social Justice 185

Index 187

About the Author 193

Introduction

"Change the World from Here" is the University of San Francisco's tagline. During the years I taught ethics classes there, I often asked students, "How does the university want to change the world?" Change, after all, can be for good or bad. We can assume that UFS assumed change for the good, but what they thought the good looked like remains an open question.

We can certainly have different definitions of the good. In fact, as I also repeated in my classes, "Most people do what they think is right (good), considering the world they think they live in." Most ethical conflicts, in other words, are not between right and wrong but between different ideas of what is right. Conflict occurs because people live in different "worlds." So, how do we change a world?

Our worlds have changed through technology, wars, climate change, migrations, and other disruptions of the status quo. Some changes have been beneficial and some not so much. Global warming appears to have the most serious consequences if we do not intervene, yet we seem more focused on social issues than collaborating to prevent further environmental destruction. This may look like a mistake, but I think it makes sense if you assume that we will only be able to deal adequately with our environmental challenges once we have dealt with the social challenges.

As long as our social climate reflects a binary ideology of "us-and-them," we will never address the climate crisis that impacts all of us. Some may escape our social ills by moving away from them, but there is no hiding from the weather, as residents of Ashville, NC recently discovered. We are in this one together, whether we like it or not.

Most of us, and our families and friends, have become vulnerable to floods, droughts, hurricanes, tornadoes, and heat waves. We are united in our vulnerability. Instead of this unity bringing us together, we are split into those who encourage environmental policies and those who try to block them. There is little agreement on how we should protect ourselves, especially those who are most vulnerable.

There is a similar disagreement about our overall national social climate, especially in the acknowledgement of the causes of our current malaise. Some appear to live in near total amnesia about the role of slave labor and stolen land in the making of American prosperity. They even continue to promote the white supremacy that resulted from the "victory" of European settlers in dominating American land and people. Others have endured struggles and hardships to safeguard vulnerable groups from exploitation and even murder, and they persistently advocate for human rights and justice.

Here is how I see it: Our European ancestors' acts of enslavement and genocide created a "climate of injustice" that has never been corrected, because doing so would have endangered American prosperity. Now American prosperity threatens our planet. We must change the current climate of injustice to a climate of justice to save the planet.

I stopped teaching in the Philosophy Department at the University of San Francisco in 2018 so I could devote myself to working out a strategy for changing our social climate from a climate of injustice to a climate of justice. Springer published *A Climate of Justice* as an open access book in 2022, thanks to LYASIS's (an organization of libraries and other information collection agencies) inclusion of the book in their series aligning with the United Nations' Global Sustainability Goals.

Before the book came out, during the COVID pandemic, I began writing posts for my *Climate of Justice Project* blog. It served as a good substitute for the classroom, with opportunities to write responses to events, books, and conversations—a continuation of my intellectual life. Special thanks to Erdmut Brown for editing and proofreading the posts for the past four years, to Mark Brown for applying his keen eye to the final draft, and to those who have made responses to the different posts and challenged my thinking.

Most of the posts were specific responses to social and political events, my readings, and reflections. A good number of the posts benefited from the ideas of other authors—almost sixty authors in total—and they are listed in the Index. Even though I learned much from their writings, I am solely responsible for my opinions.

After writing over 120 posts, I began to wonder if I had created something more than a series of posts. Last fall. I began to see that the posts could be sorted into different categories, which allowed me to see different groups of posts related to one idea or another. Finally, I saw that these categories could be seen as different steps in the work of changing the world to a climate of justice. Even though the steps came from the posts, now the posts serve as illustrations of the steps.

So, how do the 20 steps guide us toward good change? The posts are one answer. They are my responses during the 2020-to-2024 timeframe to issues and ideas that seemed to either block or promote a climate of justice. Which steps we take in the coming years depends on our discernment of the obstacles and possibilities that lie ahead.

Focus the Mind on A Climate of Justice

Climate of Justice and Climate Justice

Feb 2020

So, what's the difference between the widely used phrase "climate justice" and the climate of justice?

The climate of justice and climate justice refer to quite different areas of concern. Climate justice refers to the unequal distribution of the harms of global warming and other forms of planetary destruction. In many cases, the global economy that has caused our current climate crisis has benefited some at the expense of many others. Also, poor and many non-Western communities have fewer resources than Western communities to change their social practices, so climate justice entails helping those most impacted and least able to deal with the changing global environment.

The climate of justice, on the other hand, refers to a social context in which people intend to act with fairness toward one another and the Earth and expect to live in reciprocal relationships. In a climate of justice, people design social structures that protect the vulnerable and restrain the bullies.

The phrase climate of justice does not refer to particular actions, although a climate of justice would encourage just acts. Nor does a climate of justice refer to individual virtues, although individuals existing in a climate of justice would have a disposition toward justice since the climate itself disposes them to seek justice. It's best understood as a social context in which we expect fairness because that's what people tend to want in such situations.

The issue is straightforward: We need a climate of justice to address the escalating trends of social and planetary disintegration, but the Atlantic commerce of enslaved and dislocated people created an environment of injustice that continues to shape our context. People of privilege, of course, have adjusted to this climate because we have received more than we deserve. For others, the opposite is true. The fact is that we have never sufficiently addressed our injustices, and they now prevent us from joining together to change the current trends that are destroying our human habitat.

The Climate of Justice Project does not compete with or replace the work on climate justice. It adds another area of concern to the conversation. It examines the causes and impacts of the climate of injustice—such as white supremacy and racism—and seeks to disempower them.

Who will protect us?

May 2020

All human communities have to do three things: provide for one another, protect one another, and find social meaning. If a community does the first two well, the third is included. If it does one poorly, then the meaning of living together is fragmented and quite chaotic, as we see today in our nation.

Who is the "us" that needs protection? Some of us are doing quite well, thank you! We live in secure social worlds—with good public services, healthy populations for the most part, and financial resources. Such social worlds promote an attitude of invincibility rather than vulnerability. Others live in dangerous vulnerable social worlds. As we learned from the recent storms and fires, as well as the spread of the coronavirus, anyone could end up in either group. Still, the distinction makes sense because, in most cases, some of us have resources to protect ourselves and some do not.

The question of "Who will protect us?" draws our attention to the relationships between these two groups: the invincible and the vulnerable. What do we see? First, we notice that the relationships among the groups are social relations, not personal relations. Members of the two groups may not have any personal connection, but neither are they on separate islands without any interaction between them. Both groups depend on the same networks, infrastructures, and resources. The question is whether the social climate between the two groups represents a climate of justice or a climate of injustice?

In a climate of justice, the relationship would be based on reciprocity. The relationship would not be out-of-balance. The groups would still be different, but the invincible group would not gain from the vulnerability of others, and the vulnerable would not fear harm from the invincible group.

Some might think that protection today requires more guns, more heroes, and more wars. I want to propose a different approach. Protection requires more connection, more caring, and more community.

What I want to suggest is that the question "Who will protect us?' should direct us to our civic obligations. What do protective relationships among members of the civic look like? As I see it, the civic includes two groups: civilians who need protection and citizens who have the means to protect them. Civilian Review Boards are a good model for how these two groups are related. Civilians appeal to a board of citizens. This means that the social differences between the vulnerable and the privileged show up in the civic space as civilians and citizens, and they negotiate together how they can honor the rights of all.

Living in a Climate of Injustice

June 2020

If you ever wondered if we live in a climate of injustice, the last two months should have eliminated any doubt. The question is not whether we live in a climate of injustice, but how.

Some seem to flourish in such a climate. Trump's rally in Tulsa was only possible in a social climate in which people felt they could intimidate others, be praised for echoing Trump's hatred, and show their white arrogance without shame.

On the other hand, Black Lives Matter's call for justice, for reform, for reparation; and the abolition of white supremacy, has exposed a climate of injustice that has been taken as "normal" by too many of us, too much of the time. While city, state, and federal agencies can make institutional changes in response to civilian demands, changing the social climate to one of justice will take some time. During this time, we will continue to live in a climate of injustice.

The climate of injustice has a stubbornness that is hard to overcome. Since the European enslavement of Africans, settlement on Indigenous people's territory, and the massacre of civilians, the climate of injustice has been a necessary condition for the advancement of American prosperity. The protection of American prosperity, until this moment, has prevented us from addressing the crimes against humanity on which American prosperity rests. The result is that the strong tailwinds of the climate of injustice continue to blow us into a future that none of us want.

The Resiliency of Evil

Dec 2020

What happened? Wasn't Trump and his cohorts supposed to disappear after Biden won the election. I imagined them playing golf and then fading away as the year ended. No such luck. And that's not really the worst part. The millions who worship him are just as devoted as before the election.

It's not that easy to acknowledge that there is no "away" where we could put evil. "Away" doesn't exist. Things just go someplace else. We do try. We tried to dispense with the evil of 2 million civilians dying in Vietnam by honoring our veterans. We tried to by-pass the evil of destroying wildlife habitats by focusing on the joys of Disney World.

After the liberation movements in the 60s and 70's, reactionaries elected Ronald Reagan to block the promise of equal rights and a viable habitat. Reactionaries reappeared after the election of Barak Obama, and then ignited the embers of racism and white resentment, which carried Trump into the White House. His overt racism and white rage made Reagan look like a weasel. In fact, Trump has committed acts that should have brought him before the International Criminal Court.

Still, it would be a mistake to take Trump as the source of evil. Trump is more of a parasite than a host. He may feed off evil, but he's not the source.

So, where does this evil come from? If we did not know its source, we might say it's from some metaphysical beings such as the devil or a vengeful god. But we know the answer. It's from the Atlantic commerce of enslaved people and appropriated lands that made America what it is today. These violations of humanity created a climate of injustice that is our American context.

We have never repaired these violations of humanity, and we have not stopped them. We could get that evil off our shoulders, not by throwing it away, but rather by taking it in and making amends. So far, when people have moved in that direction, reactionaries have risen up to block their efforts, and thereby have made our evils even more resilient. If we have learned anything since the election, it is that Trump and his believers are not going away.

I didn't see it coming. And I couldn't imagine Trump totally captivating the Republican party. If it had not been for the pandemic, he might have won another 4 years. We need to be on guard. We must change the social climate—to a climate of justice—so Trumpers will stay inside.

A Promise without a Soul

July 2020

There's a battle going on, that's for sure, but is it for the "Soul of America" as Joe Biden has suggested? Let's do what we can to get Biden elected. Let's also make sure we know what we are fighting for. What we say will make a difference.

Biden appears to have gotten the idea of the American soul from Jon Meacham's book *The Soul of America: The Battle for our Better Angels* (2018).

So, what's the soul anyway? One finds an early use of the metaphor in the Biblical "J" document: "And the Lord God formed man of the dust of the ground, and breathed into his nostrils the breath of life, and man became a living soul." (Genesis 2:7)

According to this story, the first human (Adam) came from the soil (Adamah). Humans, in other words, are living creatures, and belong to the Earth—a habitat. If there is one thing you could say about United States is that it does not belong to the Earth. We not only decimated the habitats of Indigenous people; we treated and continue to treat the Earth as a commodity one can buy and sell; as real estate. There's no soul here.

Ok, Biden probably was not thinking of United States as a colonizing empire. Nor was Meacham. In his book, Meacham writes:

> In terms of Western thought, then, the soul is generally accepted as a central and self-evident truth. . . What is the American soul? The dominant feature of that soul—the air we breathe, or to shift the metaphor, the controlling vision—is the belief, as Jefferson put it in the Declaration, that all men are created equal (8-9).

One question, of course, is who is the "we" that breathes this air. Did it include Sally Hemings? Let's not forget that when Jefferson wrote the Declaration, there were almost a half million enslaved Africans creating much of the wealth that enabled the colonies to even consider independence from England. (Some even argue that the likelihood that England would abolish slavery was a key factor in deciding for independence). Does anyone see something like a "soul" here?

Meacham calls the American soul a "belief." Did Jefferson and other Anglo-Saxons really believe that all men were created equal? In any case, believing does not create a soul. Believing certainly did not create the social climate (the air we breathe) in the eighteenth century. That social climate was created by the Atlantic commerce between Europe, Africa, and the Americas.

After reading Meacham's book, one might think that the American soul refers to some core goodness that was damaged by our "lesser angles." This may remind you of the story of the Garden of Eden. I don't think this archetype fits with our history. There is no "goodness" to return to. That doesn't mean that your or my ancestors were evil, although some were. It does mean that there is no "greatness" that we could "make again." We do not have a past to return to, but a past to repair.

The language of an American soul will not get us where we need to go. The Declaration was not an expression of a belief or a truth. It was a "declaration" that declared "all men are created equal". Martin Luther King Jr. had the right metaphor when he said that the Declaration was a promissory note. In his "I have a Dream" speech, King says:

> When the architects of our republic wrote the magnificent words of the Constitution and the Declaration of Independence, they were signing a promissory note to which every American was to fall heir. This note was a promise that all men, yes, black men as well as white men would be guaranteed the unalienable rights of life, liberty, and the pursuit of happiness.

We could see the Declaration, in other words, as a "speech act," that created a promise; a promise that was made in a context of the devastation of the Earth, the displacement and killing of Indigenous people and the enslavement of Africans. It happened, in other words, in a climate of injustice that Northern and Southern states have continued through compromises to protect American Prosperity. There is no soul here, but a promise that has not yet been kept.

Why does the promise remain unfulfilled? Because we have not changed our national climate from a climate of injustice to a climate of justice. We have certainly protested against injustices, but fighting against injustice does not create a climate of justice. That requires the repair of social relations, the sharing of communal wealth, and the restoration of our natural habitat.

A Framework for Our Thinking

Nov 2021

It seems much more complicated to get out of the mess we are in than it was to get into it. You can change the game of basketball a bit, for example, on the same basketball court. If you want to change it a lot, you will have to change the court.

Instead of the common Western model of thinking in triads or threes, I propose we think in fours. Triadic thinking gives us "the economy, government, and civil society." Triadic thinking also gave us "Father, Son, and Spirit," so I don't want to eliminate it. Still, it's the framework that got us into the mess we are in. I propose a framework of "the Earth, our humanity, the social, and the civic." This framework allows me to define American prosperity in terms of four key characteristics:

- Earth is treated as a commodity
- Humans are racialized
- Social relations are dismissed and denied
- The civic is militarized.

8

And what would the transformation of American prosperity require?

- We acknowledge the Earth as a habitat for all
- We affirm each other's dignity
- We repair social relations with others.
- We protect civilians

Although those of us who have benefited from American prosperity may not feel like we have connections to the origins of the climate of injustice, we do need to examine how its benefits to us were costs to others, and how we can change our social systems so relationships are not based on winners and losers but on reciprocity.

There is much work to do. I doubt if it will get done unless we remember where we live: in a climate of injustice.

The Climate in Egypt and Qatar

Nov 2022

If you want to see what a "climate of justice" looks like, look at the COP27 meeting in Sharm El Sheikh, Egypt.

First, the rich nations agreed to put on the meeting's agenda the issue of "loss and damage." The question was how to balance the scale between those who have both caused and benefited from climate disruption and those who were innocent and had suffered.

For two weeks, the wealthy and privileged listened to representatives of hurt and vulnerable peoples. As the Prime Minister of Ireland, Michael Martin, said:

> The burden of climate change globally is falling most heavily on those least responsible for our predicament. We will not see the change we need without climate justice.

Once it was on the agenda, the call for justice could not be ignored. By the third day of the meeting, European nations had pledged millions to a "loss and damage" fund. There were also holdouts. At first the United States declined to join the other wealthy nations in supporting the fund and only on the last day did they accept such a fund.

Whether the US pays for its damages to other nations is uncertain at best. The next Republican controlled House of Representatives is unlikely to agree to send money oversees to those who have suffered from our prosperity.

The point is: The COP27 conference demonstrated what a climate of justice would entail: the privileged and the vulnerable engage in cooperative conversations about making amends for past injustices.

The World Cup, on the other hand, is taking place in a climate of injustice. Firstly, fundamental human rights are being violated. But there is more: instead of listening to the poor and vulnerable—such as migrant workers—Qatar has exploited them. Qatar has spent between 200 and 300 billion dollars building a city for the World Cup, which represents not only an unjust distribution of wealth but also an environmental disaster.

Then there is the World Cup itself. How could something be unjust when beloved by millions? Karl Marx said that religion was the opium of the people, but then he didn't know about sports.

It's easy and maybe necessary to engage in a kind of social amnesia to join in current pastimes. On the other hand, it's past time we looked at where we are headed.

These two events in the Middle East tell us a lot about the difference between a climate of justice and a climate of injustice and they also give us two models to imitate. What's our choice?

Signs of Justice

Sept 2023

How can we tell if we are moving toward a climate of justice? What are the signs we should be looking for? There are signs we are moving toward legal justice. Over a thousand people who broke into congressional buildings have been arrested. Trump faces 91 indictments, and the trials are coming. But are there signs of a desire for a climate of justice?

When we look at our social climate as a social system, then we could consider its positive and negative feedback loops. Positive feedback loops reinforce any system's direction. As they say: nothing succeeds like success. Negative feedback loops function as a drag on a system's movement.

This not only works for social systems but also for individuals. When Trump gets away with telling lies and learns that his followers increase their support, then he is encouraged to tell more (and bigger) lies. On the other hand, if there is an increasing impact from the negative consequences of lying, then the negative consequences might shut him down. I certainly hope that the courts and the rule of law will shut him down. We will find out in the coming months.

Trump is not a social system, of course, but he does represent or express a social movement that has gained momentum in the past decades. Even though it has recently experienced negative feedback, it's unclear if the dynamics indicate a change in direction or some kind of stalemate. Remember that we have never corrected the climate of injustice that emerged from our establishment of a slave colony on Indigenous people's land, so a stalemate leaves us with a climate of injustice.

However, there is no need for despair, as we are not alone in our desire and efforts to bring about a change in the climate. A clear majority do not want the future the Trump gang envisions. A majority believe that the planet cannot support his world. Perhaps we can prevent this social movement from shaping our future.

Blocking an increase of injustice, of course, is not the same as promoting justice. Fighting against injustice can sometimes be a symbol of justice, or at least a promise to uphold justice. The UAW strike against three automobile companies, for example, signifies a desire for justice: for a more equal distribution of company profits and protection of worker's rights to work. We need to remember, however, that justice resides in relationships. Corporate leaders may meet the worker's demands, but not in a climate of justice, if they refuse to cooperate in finding a just settlement and only concede as much as necessary to protect their privileges.

The empowerment of the vulnerable most clearly signifies a breakthrough to a climate of justice, especially when the relationship between the powerful and the powerless is reciprocal.

Reciprocity does not mean treating everyone the same. Differences are recognized, but the relationships are based on truth-telling, repair, and cooperation. Everyone lives in the same house, so to speak, and together they sort out who does what chores. A household based on reciprocity prevents some from gaining at another's expense, and when that has been the case, repairs are made.

As we now recognize, repairs are necessary in all our social systems, which has prompted the call for reparations. The demand for reparations signifies *justice*, but it will only become a sign of a *climate of justice* when civic leaders seek cooperative relationships with all parties.

To enable such cooperative relations, corporate leaders must relinquish what Jefferson Cowie calls in his book *Freedom's Dominion* the "freedom to dominate." Cowie focuses on the long tradition of white Southerners' resistance to federal power, but his analysis also applies to corporate leaders who resist any curtailing of their freedom to control "their" corporation.

Once corporate leaders acknowledge that their "freedom to dominate" is determined by organizational relations, not individual capacity, then it will become clear that changing their relationships with workers entails relinquishing this socially constructed freedom for the sake of cooperation. If this occurs, then cooperation among different parties would be a sign of a climate of justice, as well as a move toward creating the conditions for reversing the current trends toward an unsustainable future.

Take Care of Civic Spaces

Citizens and Civilians

Nov 2021

I know we have learned that "all humans are created equal," but we are not all born in the same social world, and our different social worlds are anything but equal. Enslaved and free persons may have been created equal, but they sure were not born in the same world.

International humanitarian law has given us some guidelines here in terms of the distinction between civilians and combatants.

Combatants may well be vulnerable, but in theory they have resources to protect themselves. Civilians do not. In fact, they have not had protection against the dangers of war—of combatants. This changed in 1949, when the International Committee of the Red Cross got nations to sign the 1949 Geneva Conventions for the protection of civilians in times of war. For the first time, civilians were not dependent on the good will of warriors but rather on their leaders obeying the rule of law.

Civilians today are not dependent on philanthropy or on the good will of others. They just ask for what they deserve as members of the civic realm: enforcement of the rule of law.

This means that the realm of the civic does not erase social injuries but rather heals them. This view of the civic comes closer to the image of a Civilian Review Board as a model for democracy instead of the Town-Hall Meeting, which assumes that everyone has an equal capacity to participate. The Civilian Review Board assumes that some are vulnerable and need protection and others can protect them.

This civilian/citizen relationship could emerge from a caring response to the social condition of refugees on our border or the demand of Black Lives Matter for police to protect their communities. The civic is not a space that ignores the plight of civilians, in other words, but rather facilitates their empowerment so their voices can bring about a climate of justice.

The social and the civic present different challenges. Increasing prosperity for all may meet the social challenge, but not the civic. The civic challenge is always the empowerment of civilians and the protection of our habitat. Democracy, in the final analysis, is dependent on empowered civilians, who can point out the repair that must happen before we can move toward a sustainable future.

The Civic and the Christian Imagination

May 2023

Some may imagine the civic as a space for doing good, which is fine if it doesn't omit social estrangements. Once we include social estrangements, however, then we must imagine how we should deal with them.

Perhaps it would help to contrast the "civic imagination," with a "Christian imagination."

Willie James Jennings gives us his perspective on a Christian imagination in his book *The Christian Imagination: Theology and The Origins of Race* (2010). For him, the "Christian imagination" emerged from the early Christen church's decision that the "church" replaced "Israel" as the holder of God's covenant. This led the church to see itself as superior to Israel, which resulted not only in a long history of antisemitism culminating in the Holocaust but also in the long history of white supremacy that led to crimes against humanity in the Americas and elsewhere.

Jennings is motivated to write this critique of the Christian imagination, I assume, because he believes there is another story of Jesus as a Jew who revealed God's intimacy (Jennings' term) for both Jews and Gentiles. He proposes that instead of separating Christianity from Judaism, Christians recognize a basic interdependence.

We should note that the Christian imagination extended beyond its relationship with Judaism to encompass its relationship with the state or Roman government. The early Jewish Christian church existed under Roman rule, and while Christians might be critical of it and rebel against it, they did not see themselves participating in it. One does not see in the Biblical tradition what I would call a "civic imagination."

The civic imagination, in fact, does not have its origin in the Biblical tradition but in classical Greek experiments in government. Aristotle thought that the civic life was the telos or purpose of human communities. First family, then clans, and then the civic. Although he did not support direct democracy, he did believe that since no one leader was perfect, it was better to have several with different views.

By no means would we want to return to classical Greece and its exclusion of non-Greeks, slaves, and women from the civic sphere. Still, if you ask about the Western source of a civic imagination, it's classical Greece. There we see participation in government rather than resistance to it.

I imagine the civic not only for Greeks, but for all, so that our social disparities are not excluded from the civic, but rather are recognized, and reconciled. This means that the civic incudes both the resourceful and the resourceless, or what I call citizens and civilians. In fact, it's the civilians (the vulnerable who need protection) who have the capacity to invite citizens (those with resources) into a climate of justice.

It may be difficult to imagine such a space, especially in the United States where the "Christian imagination" continues to see government as something to resist, as though Christians still lived under Roman rule. Instead of supporting civic organizations that are subject to government (democratic) oversight and rely on government funding, "Good" Christians create non-governmental organizations that rely on private donations. Donations are tax-deductible, which means that giving donations decreases the government's revenue. In 2021, Americans donated $484.85 billion to non-governmental organizations. Imagine what the government could have done if that money had been used to improve public entities such as our public schools, public housing, and public health.

It may make sense to see us as a "Christian nation" in the sense that we live in a legacy of the Christian imagination. This not only makes it difficult to deal with white supremacy, however, but also with the development of a civic imagination. If we cannot imagine a civic realm where social injustices are corrected, I doubt if it will happen.

Is America a Nation without a Country?

May 2023

The highly regarded writer and activist, Wendell Berry, thinks so. In his latest book, *The Need to Be Whole: Patriotism and the History of Prejudice* (2022), he addresses the problem of racial prejudice, but his primary message concerns our industrialized, urban world's dismissal of the country and the people (black and white farmers) who care for it.

Berry is not an easy person to criticize. After reading his latest book, I read *The Hidden Wound*, which he wrote as a response to the civil rights unrest in 1969, and his collection of poems in *This Day: Collected & New Sabbath Poems* (2014). He wrote some beautiful things.

He is certainly a good white guy who tries to correct the course of our current trends. I think he would probably agree that we live now in a climate of injustice, and I certainly agree that we had better gain an appreciation for the Earth as our home, but I think we live in different social worlds.

Like Berry I grew up on a farm. I know the pleasure of hard work, of doing something well, of tending to plants and to animals, and the feeling of comradery with my brothers and father when we worked together. I also left the farm as Berry did, but I did not return. Although I would not have said so at the time, I assumed that the public realm that Berry faults for being alienated from the land is the context for making the changes we must make to move from the climate of injustice to a climate of justice.

As an individual, of course, a person can do what they want, but when they assume that they have good advice to help us change course, it would be good to appreciate other social worlds beside their own.

In Berry's social world, there is racial prejudice, and before that there was Jim Crow and slavery. His settlement in Kentucky, however, may not have been as violent as the deep South. Berry draws on his experience of friendships with Black people when he was young to give us reasons to think about what he calls "degrees of prejudice." He admits that he cannot know what others were feeling, but for him, "The most regrettable cost of school segregation," he writes, "was the detriment to friendships between blacks and whites." (104). I would have thought that he would have known that segregated education cost Blacks much more than friendship with whites.

The fact is that Berry's social world was not as benign as he presents it. History professor George C. Wright, in the research for his 1990 book, *Racial Violence in Kentucky, 1865-1940,* found documentation of at least 353 lynchings in Kentucky.

In Berry's social world, the most pervasive prejudice is not racial but rather urban. It's urban people treating the country (people of the land both black and white) as inferior. For him, the Civil War represented a struggle between the patriots who stood up for their country and the nationalists who attempted to infiltrate it.

> During the war, the immediate issue for both sides was the war itself: the invasion of the South by the North. Not freedom versus slavery, but a nationalist offensive versus the defense of a homeland by people who, with some justice, thought of themselves as patriots. After the war the salient political issue was that of racial equality. That was the aim of reconstruction, but the

> conflict then was between occupation and resistance
> or subversion (264)

Berry doesn't appear to adopt the ideology of the Lost Cause, but he does seem to miss the point that by the end of the war, the war had become a fight for freedom for Black people.

On the other hand, I think Berry encourages us to acknowledge the significance of the North's invasion of the homeland of Southerners, many of whom were not owners of enslaved people. The destruction of Southern lands and Western lands during the "Indian Wars" adds weight to Berry's claim that we are a nation without a country.

Could it be that "the country" is not only in Kentucky or Nebraska? Could it also exist in urban areas? One of the terms that Berry employs in opposition to the country is the "public." He sees the "public" as alienated from the land and its people.

> It [the public] is nobody's home, and its gatekeepers
> are not filled with the spirit of welcome and hospitality.
> The freedom it offers is in fact the freedom of the
> richest and most powerful to reign and the freedom
> of the less rich and powerful to succeed as "human
> resources," perhaps highly paid, perhaps not—and,
> like all "resources" under industrial rule, to be used,
> used up, and discarded (136).

There doesn't seem to be any "country" in Berry's public realm. There is no mention of public parks, libraries, museums, schools, board walks, ice rinks, movie houses, art centers, public holidays and celebrations, street parties, music festivals, theaters, sports, community centers, hospitals, research centers, volunteer centers, nor any mention of playgrounds, dog parks, or circuses, nor demonstrations, boycotts, and sit-ins.

Public life also includes the civic realm and civic participation in shaping the urban environment. It's a place, in fact, where we could develop policies that would move us toward a climate of justice.

Civic vs Religious Disagreement

Aug 2023

It's hard to underestimate the significance of the separation between church and state. Simply put, it answers our questions about how we should live together: by civic obligations instead of religious beliefs. Or to put it another way, resolving civic disagreements does not require finding religious unity.

It appears that Christian nationalists and Trump's followers have failed to honor this principle of separation, which raises the threat of religious wars. They're not alone. It's probably true that many "nations" are guided by the religion of those in power, and many of those use religion to exercise their power. Furthermore, Christianity has served as a justification for both slavery and American imperialism, as well as for human rights and inclusion. If I would define a "good religion" and if everyone agreed with my definition, we might have a good government (according to my definition), but not a civic one.

The fact is that we don't agree on what a "good" believer believes. It's also true that debate or argument cannot resolve most religious disagreements. If someone praises God for saving their house during a storm when the storm destroyed their neighbor's house, what can you say? You could say that God doesn't save one family's home and destroy another's, but it's doubtful that your claim for consistency or logic will have much impact. What can you say to those who see global warming as part of God's plan?

Civic disagreements arise when participants have different opinions about what should be done. What should we do, for example, when stronger storms destroy more homes? Should we help people get more insurance, or build stronger houses, or move them to safer places, or develop policies that decrease carbon emissions? Should we promote electric buses, tax air travel, and shut down coal mines? Different opinions provide a chance to learn from each other.

In the civic realm, when someone disagrees with me, it's a sign that they know something I don't know. They may have different observations, values, or different assumptions. If we share these differences, disagreement can be a source of mutual learning. I have been thinking and writing about the value of disagreement from my 1967 intern year at the Evangelical Academy in Germany where I watched workers and managers working through their disagreements together to my 2014 workbook *Learning Through Disagreement*. Such learning will never occur when "others" are seen as "unsaved' or inferior.

Civic participants, of course, have their own assumptions, such as that the best decisions arise from multiple voices, good arguments make a difference, and we can learn from each other. Sharing such assumptions provides civic discourse with a basic platform for exploring the reasons for different proposals that arise from different social worlds, experiences, and reflections.

Some religious social worlds, of course, prevent such mutuality. For a true believer, some are saved, and others have fallen. In the public sphere, people interpret religious beliefs as assumptions, which are not inherently sacred. They can be changed. Even though it's not that easy to deal with the assumed privileges of Christian nationalists, it's possible to imagine a different world: a world where others know things I do not, where others have the key to the door we need to open. That's possible.

In some cases, participants cannot agree on an action because of divergent assumptions. If participants have been listening to each other, then such assumptions can be examined, appreciated, and integrated into the discourse. That may make them "all too human" for some, but just right for civic disagreements.

Cooperation vs Domination

Nov 2023

Cooperation seems so normal. When I first looked at Bernard E. Harcourt's book titled *Cooperation*, I wasn't sure it was worth a serious reading. What caught my attention was the sub-title: *A Political,*

Economic, and Social Theory. This sounded like something more than a simple request to cooperate with others. What turned out to be especially helpful was his concept of "cooperative democracy."

Most of us are familiar with cooperatives. Many of us may belong to coop credit unions, may shop at cooperative bakeries and may be members of consumer coops, such as the outdoor outlet REI. Harcourt uses these experiences as a backdrop for his social and political theory of cooperation.

I think he's right that cooperation is not a foreign concept. We know that sport teams play their best when the players work together. So do soldiers on the battlefield for that matter. Cooperation is a good strategy for winning games and wars. Even Tea Party members had to cooperate among themselves to disrupt the implementation of Obama's health care plan. In these instances, the purpose of cooperation is dominance.

In many situations, cooperation exists within what I will call "plantation logic." Plantation logic is quite simple. You get "your people" to cooperate with each other to dominate the market. Cooperation in the context of capitalism, in other words, serves the goal of domination, which means that whether cooperation makes sense depends on whether it's a winning strategy or not.

What I learned from Harcourt's book is that we could embed cooperation in democracy. In fact, democracy needs cooperation. Harcourt points out that democracy needs more than procedural principles, such as one-person-one vote or everyone having a right to vote. It also requires substantive principles, such as the principle of cooperation. Cooperation, in other words, is more than working together to get the work done. It involves treating everyone with respect and dignity as equal members of the political community. Harcourt writes:

> What cooperative democracy offers, then, is a vision of democracy that is fully democratic both procedurally and substantively, tying the notion of democratic decision making to institutions and practices that truly

make possible one-person-one-vote, equal citizenship, solidarity, and sustainability. The ambition is to put all people, including those who have traditionally been disadvantaged, in a position such that they can and do fully exercise their democratic rights (p. 189).

The logic of cooperative democracy squarely opposes the logic of the plantation. This opposition parallels the opposition between a climate of justice and a climate of injustice. Perhaps, as Harcourt suggests, our experiences with local cooperatives can provide a basis for imagining something much greater.

The Civic Context of Political Campaigns

Apr 2024

Political campaigns always occur in some context, and it turns out that the context makes quite a difference. W. Barnett Pearce, in his book *Interpersonal Communication: Making Social Worlds*, developed a communication model that I will use to explore these differences. His model includes four elements: the *world* in which communication happens, the *occasion* for it, the *relationships* among those involved, and the *self-image* of the communicator or speaker. If we imagine a civic context for political campaigns that would encourage a climate of justice, we might come up with the following picture:

The Civic Context of Political Campaigns	
<u>World</u>	<u>Occasion</u>
Civic Contest	Campaign
<u>Relationship</u>	<u>Self-image</u>
Mutual Respect	Candidate

Let's define the world of political campaigns as a contest between different persons, policies and parties to gain the votes of citizens. The occasions are various campaign events where candidates try to persuade citizens to vote for them and their policies instead of their opponents. Because the candidates participate in a civic context, they treat each other with mutual respect. The candidates can develop their self-image from the other aspects of the conversation–world, occasion, and relationships—or they can bring their own self-image into the conversation and define a world, occasion, and relationship for themselves. In such cases, it's not the context that controls the conversation, but rather the candidate.

For the sake of democracy, the civic context matters more than any candidate. The world of a political contest is different than the world of sports or horse racing. Although it's OK to steal a ball in basketball, or to lie in poker, it's not OK in a civic context. In essence, a political campaign should encourage a climate of justice rather than destroy it. That will never happen, of course, unless the candidates practice mutual respect.

Let's remember that democracy is not a monument or a memorial. It is an on-going conversation that calls for mutual respect among all who belong and want to belong to a civic context.

Our Political Climate is in Crisis

June 2024

Like the natural world, the world of politics changes temperature depending on its climate. The current heat waves, fires, and floods appear to have their counterpart in the political world of threats, lies, and lawlessness. It seems clearer than ever that we will not have the will to address our environmental crisis until we address our political crisis.

Not much matches the frequent silence about our climate crisis, in spite of its daily evidence, than the denial of our political crisis. CNN will host a presidential debate on Thursday, featuring two men who are considered equal contenders for the presidency. It's a normal presidential debate just like it's a normal summer. Temperature records are being broken, lies are being told, and it is election season again.

While the debate won't have an audience and will feature muted microphones to prevent contestants from interrupting each other, it will otherwise be a typical debate. The political climate, however, is anything but normal. We have never had a debate like this before. What should we call it: "The bully and the guardian," or "The concerned and the reckless."

Just as we ignore the continual warming of the planet at our peril, so also do we ignore the changes in our political climate. Instead of increasing our sense of a civic space based on a shared humanity, we are moving further away from a climate of justice where past injustices would not be ignored but repaired.

It's a mistake to respond to this threat by only protecting the status quo. The climate of injustice we inherited from our past has not yet been corrected. Instead of merely defending our civic space, we need to improve it by making it more inclusive, equal, and reparative.

Let's face it. Justice—based on human dignity—has never been a major part of our national narrative. It has never reached the status of freedom, domination, competition, or prosperity. (It's "Life, Liberty, and the Pursuit of Happiness." Not justice.)

The 14th Amendment changed that. "Equal protection under the law" created the promise of a climate of justice—based on equal dignity. A promise we need to redeem.

And we need to do it now. We will never develop an adequate response to our environmental crisis until we begin to repair our social injustices. They are two sides of the same coin. How about a "coin of the realm" that would show how justice and sustainability belong together. Creating such a coin could symbolize an improvement in our political climate.

Time for a Civic Conscience

Oct 2024

If one's "conscience" refers to one's awareness or focus, then there doesn't seem to be much space or time in this campaign for a "civic conscience." Still, we need a clear call to a civic conscience, which neither candidate is making.

In Sheldon Wolin's classic book on political theory, *Politics and Vision*, he concludes his arguments with the call: "In the era of Superpower, the task is to nurture the civic conscience of society."

What we are aware of, pay attention to, what we see, as well as what escapes our attention, or is beyond our grasp, depends on the "world" in which we live. So, the first thing we can say is that a person acquires a civic conscience by living in the world of the civic, which is different from the world of economics or even the world of sports.

If we say that a civic conscience is like a civic perspective, then how does one acquire a particular perspective? By living in a particular world. In a capitalistic world, for example, one looks at things from one's self-interest. What's in it for me? A civic perspective is quite different. It looks at things not as a dealer or trader but as a citizen—a member of the civic. Wolin describes citizenship as follows:

> . . . citizenship provides what the other roles [in society] cannot, namely an integrative experience which brings together the multiple role-activities of the contemporary person and demands that the separate roles be surveyed from a more general point of view. It means further that effort be made to restore the political art as that art which strives for an integrative form of direction, one that is broader than that supplied by any group or organization. It means finally that political theory must once again be viewed as that form of knowledge which deals with what is general and integrative to men, a life of common involvement (p. 389).

The civic perspective, in other words, looks at society from the perspective of commonality. When we take on the role of citizen, we examine social conflicts and movements—even economic developments—in terms of their role in moving all of us toward a shared future.

A civic perspective, in other words, looks at the economy in terms of our common wealth. We are all contemporaries. This is our time. The purpose of the economy is to effectively and carefully harvest what the earth provides and then to transform these gifts into provisions for our communities.

Most of the time our perspectives emerge from our work and friendship relationships, our organizations and communities and our educational institutions—the different worlds we live in. Every once in a while, there is a call to consciously look at things from a civic perspective. One of those days is certainly the day we vote for those who represent us—those who represent us as democratic citizens.

Guard against Authoritarian Zealots

Trump's America

June 2020

Indeed, the over 100,000 deaths paint a clear picture of Trump's America, particularly when we consider the thousands of lives he could have spared if he had been performing his duties. The picture of the white police officer pushing his knee on George Floyd's neck, however, gets to the heart of the matter. Can you hear "Let's make America white again" churning in this white man's head?

Trump didn't create white supremacy or even white hatred of blacks. Instead of banishing white hatred from the public realm, however, Trump encourages it. His hatred toward Barack Obama is not so much the tip of the iceberg as the bottom of a volcano that spews hot lava. He didn't create the volcano; he fires it up.

So, what can we do? As a white male, I enjoy certain privileges, but I, along with many other white men, refuse to put our knees on a black man's neck. There are white men who are capable of doing so. More than one might think. Civilian Review Boards and other citizen groups must get these men out of public service.

My guess is that if you asked the members of any police department to identify those who are blatantly racist, you would know who should be removed from public office. Police officers probably already know who these men are. We may not be able to eradicate white racism from our communities, but we certainly can from public service and the civic sphere.

Some cities have had extensive anti-racism programs but removing racist officers has not been as widespread as it could have been. Sometimes, police unions have made it impossible. In such situations, Civilian Review Boards should first turn their attention to the members of police unions. Reforming Civilian Review Boards is also necessary in certain cases.

Cleaning out the white racists in our police departments could change the social context or climate of injustice in which we live, since it would demonstrate the use of ethical standards in the public realm.

Trump's America exudes a climate of injustice that has no limits. He has encouraged a new generation of white male haters that will be difficult to contain. We may not be able to change their hearts, but we can exclude them from our institutions. One of the basic rights of civilians is protection. That's protection by the police, not from the police!

One might think that the Republican Party would have excluded Trump from becoming their candidate in 2016. That could be a reasonable expectation if this private organization had any ethical standards to evaluate people who wanted to join their party. So, we have a white racist in the White House, and it's our task to remove him in the next election.

We must take America away from Trump. We will not do this by calling for a return to some previous America. We have always been a nation steeped in racism, to varying degrees. We must repair the past, not repeat it. None of this is possible, however, unless we work first on voter registration and then on winning the election.

What Kind of Trouble Are We In?

Sept 2020

We are in trouble. Is it "good trouble" as advocated by John Lewis, or some other kind?

Are we heading toward something like the "troubles" in Ireland: bombings, assassinations, fires, torture? Will we become terrified instead of just fearful?

Or is it like the trouble in the French town of Calais during the Hundred Years War when the British laid siege to the town and six leading citizens surrendered to save it; immortalized in Rodin's sculpture, "The Burghers of Calais"?

What about the troubles that echo loudly in American history?

Nobody knows the trouble I've been through

Nobody knows my sorrow

Nobody knows the trouble I've seen

Glory hallelujah!

For some of us, troubles are no stranger. Some troubles, of course, were created and maintained by us—the white male social world in which I, and many of you, exist. At times, it seems like we have moved beyond these troubles, and then they appear again.

Given the white male dominance of our nation right now, we face two troubles: troubles that are denied and ignored, and troubles that are shattering our mirror of ourselves. You know the first kind: the troubles caused by our wanton expansion of capitalism, or what I prefer to call "American prosperity." We are destroying our own habitat. We are turning away from the millions of economic and environmental refugees and violating their human rights and our sense of a shared humanity. Thousands die while we play on the beach.

If we are to address these troubles, we must confront what has become too obvious to ignore: the secession of the Executive Branch, and much of the Republican Party, from the Union.

This conflict is not between the states but rather between the branches of government and the people themselves. Trump has taken over the Executive Branch, for the most part, and has weakened the Supreme Court's capacity to limit his control of the election. The Republican Party, loyal to Trump's reign, has the Senate do his bidding. In contrast to the Southern states' secession, this secession has not been a separation from the Union to form a separate nation, but rather a secession to dominate the entire nation.

This is big trouble, and I don't think it's good. "Good trouble" shakes things up, unfreezes things, so they can be put together better. Bad trouble shakes things up so some can gain more power over others. Terrible trouble shakes things up, so they fall apart. Some on the far left and far right might vote for terrible trouble, but they ignore how many of us depend on the rule of law to protect us. Laws need to be changed—that's the role of good trouble—but not eliminated.

This could be the time of terrible trouble. I'm terrified. Therefore, it is imperative that we engage in and support voting like never before. We can no longer ask for the government to unite the people; the people have to unite the government.

Christian Zionism and American "Civil Religion"

Mar 2024

It could be that our government continues to ship bombs to Israel because we, like Israel, are a settler nation. In different ways—Jews were indigenous to Palestine and Europeans were not indigenous to the Americas—Israel and the United States use the same Biblical stories to provide cover for the displacement and massacre of Indigenous people.

The best-known source of the notion of "civil religion," in the United States is Robert Bellah's essay *Civil Religion in America* (1967). He doesn't include the Second Coming, but he refers to the Bible, ignores indigenous Americans, and assumes that the land belongs to European settlers. He writes:

> Until the Civil War, the American civil religion focused
> above all on the event of the revolution, which was

30

seen as the final act of the Exodus from the old lands across the rivers. The Declaration of Independence and the Constitution were the sacred scriptures and Washington the divinely appointed Moses who led his people out of the hands of tyranny.

Christian evangelicals have transformed this "civil religion" into political propaganda as demonstrated by Vice President Pence's speech in the Knesset in 2018:

> In the story of the Jews, we've always seen the story of America. It is a story of an exodus, a journey from persecution to freedom, the story that shows the power of faith and the promise of hope. My country's very first settlers also saw themselves as pilgrims, sent by Providence, to build a new Promised Land. (quoted in Mitri Raheb *Decolonializing Palestine,* 2023)

As the Christian Palestinian theologian Mitri Raheb explains:

> The bond between the State of Israel and the United States is of a strategic political and military nature and is grounded in the common belief of being a chosen people as a settler community called to rule (p. 114).

Our "civil religion" and Christian Zionism have one more thing in common. The settlement of Israel and settlement of the United States created a "climate of injustice" that they both deny. If we desire a climate of justice the first step is to recognize the origins of the climate of injustice in which we live today.

A Message to Christian Nationalists

July 2024

If I understand you correctly, you want to do "God's will," and that you know "God's will" from the Bible, which is "God's Word." In terms of different theories of interpretation, your view would be called an "originalist theory of interpretation."

This theory assumes that you can understand a text without understanding its context. Or, to put it another way, to understand a ship in a bottle, ignore the bottle and focus exclusively on the ship. If every text exists in some context—it was written at some time and some place—and if you assume that the context does not matter, then you must assume that we still live in the 1st century during the time of the Roman Empire

Some interpreters have done a masterful job of taking the text (ship) out of the 1st century context (bottle) and applying it to a 21st century context (bottle), but not with an originalist theory of interpretation. Instead of disregarding the context, these interpreters rely on the social context to reveal the text's meaning, or more accurately, they engage in a dialogue between the text and the context.

This becomes particularly significant when considering our democratic context. If you examine the Bible closely, there is precious little about democracy. You have kingdoms and empires. Jerusalem was part of the Roman Empire in the first century. Jesus never said a word about equal representation or the right to vote. The first century bottle is filled with many stories and experiences, but not with democracy.

Some argue that Christian nationalism is not democratic and even anti-democratic. If you stay in the original Biblical bottle, you are probably both.

Who has been Chosen?

Sept 2024

If God were a just God who created everyone, it would seem strange for God to favor some people over others. Or, to put it another way, a just God would not violate the basic principle of justice by favoring some over others. Doesn't that make sense, even if you are a believer?

You may think that only believers should talk about God, but some use their theology to do so much harm in the civic sphere, I don't think we can leave theology up to them. We all have a stake in the ideas that enter the civic realm. So, I would like to engage in what I call a "post-Christian theology." It's "post-Christian" because it moves beyond the Christian ideology that God has chosen some over others to carry out God's work.

It's important to bring this up because some of Trump's followers believe that God has chosen him to become President of the United States. They see confirmation of this belief in the turning of his head to miss the bullet that was aimed at him.

Now, if we lived in the 1st century and were tribal members, we might have assumed that our God would protect us, especially the leaders of our tribe. Actually, that's what tribal gods did. Living in the 21st century, however, where we understand justice as respecting the human dignity of each person, it doesn't make sense to think that God would choose some over others. So even if you believe that God turned Trump's head when the bullet whizzed by, God would have done the same for anyone else.

If we want to move toward a climate of justice, we need to affirm the idea of a just God who does not choose Christians over Jews, Israel over Palestinians, or Trump over Harris. Who has been chosen? No one, or we could say everyone. Any God worth having, in other words, would never violate basic principles of justice.

Honor our Human Dignity

To be Born or Created

Feb 2021

What would you think of changing the name of the Golden State Warriors to the Golden State Troupe (troupe, not troopers)? Can we de-militarize and de-racialize our professional sports and see them as players? That's probably a small change compared to thinking about ourselves as "born" rather than "created." Let's start with the Declaration of Independence.

> We hold these truths to be self-evident, that all men are created equal, that they are endowed by their Creator with certain unalienable Rights, that among these are Life, Liberty and the pursuit of Happiness.

Compare that with the beginning of the United Nations Declaration of Human Rights:

> Whereas recognition of the inherent dignity and of the equal and inalienable rights of all members of the human family is the foundation of freedom, justice and peace in the world,

Is there an "inherent dignity" that must be respected and that belongs to "all members of the human family/" Would not this "inherent dignity" be a "birthright?" Humans have dignity, in other words, because they are living beings.

We are living beings who live through participation in the biosphere: through breathing. The air circulates in and out of our bodies and as long as that happens, we live our lives. The cry, "I can't breathe" exposes our connection to our shared habitat. When our caretakers help us begin to breathe, I believe we become fully human and have the birthright to be respected.

Choosing to be born rather than created has a couple of advantages. It fits with our experience. We are born of a woman. We are born into a family and rely on that family for our existence. We experience the worthiness of babies when we make eye contact with them. Even though we are born into very different social worlds, we are all equal when we take our first breath.

The idea that we are created, of course, assumes a Creator, and almost without exception, this Creator has national preferences. Whether we choose our birth or our creation as the basis of equality, of course, cannot erase our vast inequalities. On the other hand, it would be hard to argue that some newborns have less worth than others. The admirable charities and philanthropists who provide aid to children throughout the world testify to our basic equality.

I think that seeing our dignity grounded in our being human would help us move toward a climate of justice because it bypasses religious conflicts and wars, it recognizes our connection to the planet, it honors our parents and caregivers, and it gives each one of us our due. We don't need a Creator to have dignity; it comes with our birth. That's why we celebrate "Birthday" rather than "Creation Day."

Putin's humanity

Apr 2022

What happened to Putin's humanity or the soldiers who killed for sport in Bucha? Their behavior seems to resemble that of a psychopath. The web site, *Psychopathy*, which aims to dispel myths and share research on this condition, suggests three symptoms: an uncaring temperament, boldness and social dominance, and disinhibited behavior. Sounds about right.

These conditions, of course, do not make someone a killer of civilians.

We always live in some world and these worlds are maintained by the stories we tell. The stories do not have to be true, as Trump followers have shown us. Some worlds allow, or at least do not prevent, crimes against humanity. That's the world we live in today. This world has been a long time coming, and it has now made possible the destruction of our human habitat. If Putin were a duck, our world would be his waterway. If you give 10 children a gun, how many will shoot you? What happens if you give them dolls?

There are more causes than one's "world," there is also one's agency. Putin decided to do this. He could have done otherwise. That's what makes his crimes incomprehensible. How could someone decide to bomb hospitals and train stations?

How could a human being who is being human do what Putin is doing? We could, of course, ask a similar question of many others. Let's reflect on Thomas Jefferson for a minute. He was not Putin, but he was an enslaver, raped young black women, bred enslaved people for profit, and he also wrote The Declaration of Independence. How should we understand that? Was he a genius in creating totally separate compartments for his different behaviors? Was there a "basic" humanity deeper than all his desires and behaviors? Did he still have the possibility of being a witness to his own dignity, or had it been destroyed?

Can one lose consciousness of oneself as a living being, as a part of a vibrant, larger whole? It seems so. It does make sense that committing crimes against humanity has consequences for one's own humanity. Or is a loss of consciousness of one's humanity necessary to commit crimes against humanity? Is it possible to create such a vibrant, larger whole where such crimes are impossible? How could we move in that direction?

The first obligation, of course, is to stop the killing and to hold the killers accountable. We could also take some time to examine how our policies are true to our humanity. As you know, we don't live in a climate of injustice because of Putin, but because of violations of our shared humanity. Acknowledging these violations and addressing them may be a necessary step toward creating a world where our humanity is protected rather than threatened.

Human Dignity and Civic Spaces

May 2022

It's becoming clearer than ever that allowing God to enter the civic realm causes a lot of trouble. The separation of church and state has been violated so much that now the President talks about our nation's "soul" (nation states may have a social context or climate—a climate of injustice—but that does not constitute a soul). Furthermore, our Catholic Supreme Court justices now seem intent on obeying their version of God's laws rather than our civic laws.

Let's not forget the reason for the separation of church and state. It was instituted to prevent religious wars. Follow whatever religious doctrine you want, but do not use civic laws to force others to agree with you. When our government in the 1950's defined the fight against Communism as a religious war instead of a conflict between capitalism and socialism, our civic sphere was compromised. And it's been downhill from there. The civic realm may be "all too human," as some lament, but bringing God to the rescue has only made things worse.

This does not mean that religious beliefs cannot be a source of what it means to be human or what we should share. Simply put, a civic

37

perspective on human nature remains independent of any particular religious ideology, even though it may draw inspiration from multiple religious ideologies. Because the civic is not created or maintained by the gods, their representatives should not rule the civic, but they may bring enlightenment to the civic. The Rev. Martin Luther King Jr., for example, believed as a Christian that we are all God's children, but he did not lead a new Christian movement. He led a civil rights movement.

The title of King's speech in Memphis in February 1968 was, "All Labor has Dignity." The background of King's view of dignity was certainly the Christian religion, but it was also the philosophy of personalism that he studied in graduate school. In any case, the idea of human dignity served as the basis for the UN Declaration of Human Rights. It does seem possible to free the source of dignity from religious beliefs and to ground it in our humanity.

We can witness our human dignity in our purposeful vitality, which the neurobiologist, Antonio Damasio, calls the "core self." Neurons create maps in the brain that then produce mental images of us as living beings. How could it get better than that?

My guess is that most mothers know this. A newborn is a sight to behold. As a father, I also know something about this. (I believe that some other primates share similar experiences.) When I put on my theological hat, I could see where religious language could help to interpret this experience, but I don't believe it is necessary. Our experience of our bodies reveals on a very simple level a human dignity that both brings enjoyment and needs protection.

What I don't understand are parents who seem to allow their religious beliefs to get in the way of enjoying and honoring not only their bodies but also the body of others. In a free country, they may have the right to do so, but they certainly do not have the right as citizens to force others to accept their religious beliefs.

As we all know, the Catholic church has a miserable history of oppressing women with their religious beliefs, and other Western religions are not much better. In any case, we now have a Supreme Court dominated by Catholics, who seem to follow their religious beliefs about the place and function of women in the world and deny them their fundamental human dignity.

An important tenet of our democracy is the separation of church and state, which has been violated in multiple ways by different groups, but even more fundamental for a sustainable democracy is the protection of each person's human dignity.

In the coming election, we will not be able to change the Supreme Court, but we can save our democracy if we want to.

Our Shared, but Not Common Humanity

Oct 2023

Central to the development of a climate of justice is the discernment that we are all equal in different ways. In a sense, only when we see each other as other—as different—can we treat each other equally. More complicated than one might expect. The long history of one group claiming superiority over another group is a history of domination of the more powerful over the less powerful. Because of this history, as an African American woman told me years ago, we do not have a "common humanity," but rather a "shared humanity."

At the time, I thought I had some idea of what she meant, but the meaning gained more significance when I recently visited the exhibit at the De Young Museum of Kehinde Wiley's *An Archeology of Silence*. As Claudia Schmuckli writes in the exhibit's accompanying book "the people in *An Archeology of Silence* force viewers to reckon with their humanity."

It forces each of us to reckon with our humanity, because as Kehinde Wiley says of his work: "Art gives me the power to imagine a set of alternative realities." These "alternative realities," I think, are alternative ways of being human.

There are many things to say about Wiley's paintings and sculptures, including that they are detailed and specific. "Humanity" is not an idea here. It is embodied in Black bodies in pain, in grief, and at rest. When I visited the exhibit, my humanity was embodied in my white body in the darkened rooms of Wiley's art.

My white body does not share the pain, the grief, nor the rest with the people in *An Archaeology of Silence*. I do recognize that I am in the presence of truth—a truth about domination, violence, and death. The implicit inhumanity of white terrorism, lynchings, and murder permeates the room, not explicitly depicted in the paintings or sculptures.

As I have reflected on my visit to the museum, I think that Wiley has magnificently presented the humanity of the lived experience of Black people as an "alternative reality." Most white people, including me, have little in common with these human experiences. Still, white visitors can share in the sadness, grief, and beauty that his art represents, and in so doing, they can share a humanity that does not deny our differences.

Protect the Earth

Why has the Environmental Movement failed us?

Apr 2020

It's not clear what question Michael Moore's new film, "Planet of the Humans," is trying to answer, but a good guess would be that it is a question about the failure of the environmental movement to save the planet. This assumes, of course, that the environmental movement has failed, but when one considers our current climate crisis, that's not unreasonable. It depends on your expectations. In any case, Moore's film gives what I see as an unsatisfactory answer.

I don't totally agree with Tom Athanasiou's assessment that the movie is "crap," but it certainly does not rise to the level of Michael Moore's best work. (Tom is an advocate for environmental justice, you can read the review on his web site: ecoequity.org.)

In the movie, Jeff Gibbs walks us through his interpretation of the promise and hypocrisy of the renewable energy movement. At first, he seems to argue that the environmental movement failed due to partnerships with corporations in the construction of large-scale solar and wind installations, which require more energy from fossil fuels for construction than they deliver from renewable sources. This is a factual question, of course, and Tom Athanasiou argues that Gibbs needs to do his homework, which could include in my opinion, the work of such organizations as the "Climate Equity Reference Project." In any case, the real reason for the failure of the renewable energy movement, according to Gibbs, is that it fails to address the more decisive issues of population growth and human nature. It turns out that both issues are not all that decisive.

For decades, population growth has been clearly identified as a red herring. We will probably see around 10 to 11 million inhabitants on the planet, and then the number will level off. Could be less. In any case, such a number will not smother the Earth.

The other "reason" for our predicament, according to this film, is human nature. Gibbs pulls out the old Western male mythology of men refusing to accept limits because of the fear of death. This is not human nature, but a Western social world with roots in monotheism, radical individualism, and Eurocentrism. Modern neurobiology and attachment theory provide a very different picture of human nature. Like other primates we seek relational security.

Humans are more complicated because our social lives are largely shaped by the stories in which we live. We need to tell a different story. I think we need to tell the story of the Atlantic commerce that created a climate of injustice that has never been corrected. It needs to include the crimes against humanity that occurred in the colonization and establishment of the American empire.

This story is not the same as that of environmental justice, which is concerned with the equitable distribution of responsibility for creating a livable habitat. Not unlike Gibbs, I also recognize our apparent inability to create appropriate limits to live among others on this one Earth. I believe we need to locate this inability not in human nature but in the white man's fear of confronting and repairing the harm caused by the drive for American prosperity—a climate of injustice.

Earth Day 2020 and the Coronavirus

April 2020

In Richard Powers novel *The Overstory*, the character Patricia, standing in front of a grove of trees, expresses her gratitude for the gifts of nature:

> Thank you for the baskets and the boxes. Thank you for the capes and hats and skirts. Thank you for the cradles. The beds. The diapers, Canoes, Paddles, harpoons, and nets. Poles, logs, posts. The rot-proof shakes and shingles. The kindling that will always light. . .. Thank you for the tools, The chests. The decking. The clothes closets. The paneling. I forget . . . Thank you" she says, following the ancient formula. "For all these gifts that you have given." And still not knowing how to stop, she adds, "We're sorry. We didn't know how hard it is for you to grow back." (p. 135)

I found this quite meaningful when I first read it, but that was before the coronavirus pandemic. It fit with my musings about our intimate relationship with the Earth.

As I see it, human life begins with our participation in the biosphere, when air enters our bodies, and it breathes us. I know, it seems like we breathe it, but that is a rather egocentric way of seeing things. Instead, it looks like humans live through their participation in the biosphere, just like fish live through their participation in water.

So, what does it mean that the coronavirus disrupts our breathing and in many cases stops it? We have used thousands of ventilators and millions of masks to maintain our breathing and to continue our participation in the Earth's biosphere, but many of us have been unable to do so. What can I say? Not so much right now. It does make sense to acknowledge that grieving is not the same as gratitude.

We are not the only primates who grieve. However, we appear to be unique in creating social worlds that remove us from the earthly context of our bodies—the source of life itself. I hope our experiences of the coronavirus will correct this misperception.

We exist as parts of larger wholes, and the parts ultimately depend on the whole. The whole is not simply our biological or social life. It's both. Still, we begin with breathing, and we end when it stops. Between our beginning and our end, we coexist on a planet that we continue to poison and exploit, and it's important to acknowledge that we have no control over the Earth's rhythms and patterns. Sometimes, they can be deadly, and we need to protect ourselves from them. Today, it still makes sense to be grateful for the Earth's provisions, but we should also be grateful to, and never forget, all those who have stood up to protect us.

Protecting the Earth's Integrity

Nov 2022

To create a sustainable future, we had better learn how to protect the Earth's integrity. We could start by understanding what violating its integrity looks like.

When I was a boy in Western Nebraska, I heard farmers talking about "turning over" pastures for planting wheat the following season. This Earth had been prairie forever (or at least a long time), and now a plow would "turn over" the Earth, so the grass would be under dirt, and the dirt would be "topsoil" for farming. Was this a violation of the Earth's integrity? The famous naturalist, John Muir fought to expel all Indigenous communities from what he perceived as "wilderness." Did he protect or violate the Earth's integrity?

Years ago, cities in the East Bay filled in the marshes around the Bay for urban growth and expansion. When the early settlers treated the Earth as real estate, as a commodity that you could buy and sell, and as an investment, did they violate the Earth's integrity? These are not frivolous questions. How we deal with them may well determine the life our grandchildren will inherit. So, let's think about it a bit more.

Something has integrity when its parts fit together to benefit the whole. Contrary to Muir's notion of wilderness, humans are part of the whole. Even our integrity, if I got this right, depends on our protection of the Earth's integrity.

You don't have to agree with the Gaia hypothesis that the Earth is a self-regulating system to agree that the Earth's integrity depends on the balancing of its parts. Photosynthesis is a good example. Plants and animals restore for each other the air they need to flourish. Human animals have now ruined this balance to our detriment.

As I see it, even though we may own private property, such as a house, I think that the private ownership of the Earth violates the Earth's integrity because the Earth should be shared with others. Given our current urban settings, taxes on land and estate taxes may help to restore the Earth's integrity, but we have not witnessed that yet.

Owning land—"This is my land"—should be a metaphor for being a steward of the Earth. If the term loses its metaphorical status and is used literally, then the integrity of the Earth is violated. The fact is that we live today in violation of the Earth's integrity. It is part and parcel of our climate of injustice. In the final analysis, the Earth does not belong to us, we belong to the Earth's living systems.

I acknowledge the Christian rebellion against the Earth. "We do not belong to it, we belong to God." It's true, the Christian god is not a fertility god but a nomadic god. He is above the Earth, not part of it. At the same time, this God, at best, cares for the vulnerable, and no one is more vulnerable today than the Earth. I think it's folly to think that any god (worth the name) would save their people and let the Earth go to hell. Even the gods, in other words, would not violate the Earth's integrity.

Why do we exist?

Mar 2023

Perhaps it was an accident. Evolution simply did not know when to stop. The planet appears to have been fine without us. There were plenty of other animals to keep the vital exchanges of carbon and oxygen in balance. Did the Earth really need us?

It could be, of course, that the gods were lonely. When you think about it, the gods (especially monotheistic gods), seem to be overly concerned about human behavior. What would the gods do if they could not fret over our fate? I don't know, but I don't think we exist to be God's playmates.

Maybe we exist to be each other's playmates. We certainly need each other to play, to protect, to provide and to love. We exist for each other. That's a no-brainer. But that doesn't answer the original question: why do humans exist? Is there a place for us in the larger scheme of things?

When one looks at our situation, maybe we exist today to clean up the mess we have made. Our children must worry about what is in store for them. Who else can decrease carbon emissions, restore grasslands, revive endangered species, care for the houseless, stop the wars, protect the children, and catch the criminals? There's lots to do.

Perhaps we created such a sorry state for our children because we either didn't know or were mistaken about why we exist. For some time now, the idea has been that we exist to build, to innovate, to "go to the moon" so to speak. Now we know that this was a narcissistic illusion. Our "pioneer spirit" is pushing us over a cliff. There's another idea. We exist to weed the flowers. OK, hogs can do that too.

There's another idea, inspired from Robin Wall Kimmerer's book, *Braiding Sweetgrass*. She writes that we have a special gift.

> Other beings are known to be specially gifted, with attributes that humans lack. Other beings can fly, see at night, rip open trees with their claws, make maple syrup. What can humans do? We may not have wings or leaves, but we humans do have words. Language is our gift and our responsibility. I've come to think of writing as an act of reciprocity with the living land. Words to remember old stories, words to tell news ones, stories that bring science and spirit back together to nurture our becoming people made of corn (347).

People of the Corn. As Kimmerer points out, corn is a cultivated crop. It doesn't grow by itself. It grows in a reciprocal relationship with humans. Corn needs us as we need corn. Why do we exist? We exist to cultivate the earth.

Cultivating the Earth may seem foreign to some city folks. Perhaps we could practice by cultivating a taste for a special food. Then we might turn to cultivating a relationship with another person. Maybe we could even cultivate a climate of justice; in such a climate, imagine all of us belonging to the Earth. Then, if we were to sit together for a meal, we might share stories of the destruction of our shared habitat and efforts to preserve it.

Critically Value the Law

A Climate of Justice and the Rule of Law

Jan 2020

So, what is the difference between a climate of justice and a climate of injustice? One difference is that in a climate of injustice, people act with impunity and flout the rule of law. In a climate of justice, people are held accountable, and people enforce laws.

Our legal code was written in a climate of injustice—caused by the enslavement, genocide, and displacement of millions in the Atlantic commerce—and the task of this project is to understand how to switch to a climate of justice—but that does not mean that the rule of law cannot serve as a source for the protection of civilians.

If Trump and his party override the rule of law, the danger increases not only for civilians—those who are vulnerable and depend on the rule of law for their protection—but also for citizens who work for justice.

Protecting the rule of law is not sufficient to create a climate of justice, but it is necessary.

My Interview with Amy Coney Barrett

Oct 2020

This interview may seem a bit strange since I composed the whole thing myself.

Your nomination to the Supreme Court raises some interesting questions. Do you think God wants you to join the Supreme Court?

I think so.

Does it matter how you got there?

What do you mean?

In Catholic ethical theory, one can justify the means if the end is a greater good than the harm of the means.

That's right. It's the end that matters—unless the means to that end are really bad.

And you don't see Trump's behavior as really bad?

It is what it is.

As a judge, I assume you pray that your decisions are correct.

Of course.

And do you get any guidance in your prayers?

You mean on particular cases?

Yes.

No, I am an originalist and follow what the text says.

So, you do not expect your prayers to make any difference?

This doesn't seem like a good question.

OK, as an originalist, what do you think of the 14th Amendment?

"Equal protection under the law" is fundamental to our democracy.

I agree, but why did the Constitution need to be amended?

I don't know what you are getting at.

Well, an originalist believes that the Constitution should be read in terms of what the authors intended. They did intend to count enslaved people as 3/5th of a person, but I doubt if they intended "equal protection under the law," or even the 19th Amendment for that matter.

I see.

Actually, it was the Republican Party that passed the 14th Amendment without the consent of the representatives of the slave states, such as your family's state of Louisiana.

And your point?

As an originalist, are you against "amending" the Constitution?

No, no; that would be going too far.

What about the idea of the Equal Rights Amendment?

I don't think I can answer that since I am not writing this interview.

Fair enough.

OK, let's turn to your attendance at the Rose Garden. You did not wear a mask. Would you have worn one if everyone else had?

I suppose so.

But you didn't. Even after the ceremony, you did not put on a mask. Do you agree with the CDC guidelines?

Yes, of course.

I know you have had the virus and are perhaps immune, but would you have worn a mask if the President had asked you to?

Of course.

Does this mean that you tend to do what the president wants?

That's not a good question.

OK, have you heard of the idea that you should dance with the person who brought you?

Yes,

So, who brought you?

President Trump

So, should you dance with him?

No, in this case, I don't think so.

Let me put it another way. What groups do you belong to?

My family, my church, my professional associations. Is that what you mean?

Not exactly. There are some groups we belong to not by how we see ourselves but rather by how others see us. Others see me as a male, as white, as privileged and so on. I assume that others see you as a teacher, mother, legal scholar, and so on. Does that make sense?

Of course.

Well, it appears that your journey to this nomination belongs to a larger story of a group of powerful conservative men who have used their money and influence to protect their privileges. I don't know if you chose this group, but it appears that the group has chosen you, which in my eyes, makes you a member. The only question is what kind of member you will be.

I think I am an independent judge.

I think that such statements can only come from members of privileged social groups that allow us to say such things. The groups that brought you to the dance, in other words, probably assumed that you would take such a position.

Well, I think I am my own person.

Right, I must ask you one last question. I promise. What do you think of the idea of a climate of justice?

I don't understand it.

It's about our social climate or context in which we make decisions. The argument is that we now live in a climate of injustice, where some have more at the expense of others, and we must change this climate before we can create a viable future.

I think that's above my pay grade.

The Rule of Law vs the Law of Rule

May 2022

The Supreme Court's draft statement on abortion clarifies an issue I have thought a lot about when writing *A Climate of Justice*: "Can civilians depend on the enforcement of the rule of law?" I guess they cannot, and neither can we.

Because of the world-wide agreement that civilians have a right to protection in times of war, one could have hoped that civilians were not dependent on the generosity of persons but on the law for their protection. I knew that laws had to be enforced, but I assumed that civilians could at least make an appeal that they should be enforced. Laws, in other words, were not descriptive statements of current relations but rather normative statements that give us a lodestar to change current relations.

I knew that laws had been used to justify slavery and segregation, as well as allowed lynching and white terrorism. At the same time, laws had been used to protect workers from harm and children from abuse. There are laws "on the books" that are the result of courageous struggles for civic and human rights. Trump, Putin, and now the Supreme Court have shown us how tenuous it is to ensure that what we write turns out to be right.

The hallmark of a constitutional democracy is that no one is above the law, which also means that no one is below the law. Laws, in other words, should not be used as instruments of oppression, which is what the Supreme Court is set to do. They can do this because the majority lied during a Congressional confirmation process and now rule the roost.

Where does that leave us? It leaves us with the only thing we have left: the ballet box. This election is not just about democracy or autocracy; it's also about the rule of law or the law of rule. No one is safe until we restore the legal foundation of democracy.

How can Catholics become Originalists?

Sept 2023

Maybe a weird question until you remember that the US Supreme Court is dominated by Catholic originalists. Now that is something to ponder! This is worth pondering, at least from my perspective, because recent decisions by the Supreme Court have not promoted a climate of justice, but in fact, the opposite. Their decisions on such issues as abortion, affirmative action, *Citizens United*, discrimination, and voting rights have pushed "liberty and justice for all" further away.

As the law professor Erwin Chemerinsky argues in his book *Worse Than Nothing: The Dangerous Fallacy of Originalism* (2022), they have used the theory of originalism as a blanket to cover-up their ultra-conservative values.

The theory of originalism holds that the founder's intention, and/or what the text says, determines the meaning of the Constitution. Instead of trying to legislate laws, the originalist justices apply the laws as they were written by the writers who wrote them. For example, as Chemerinsky points out, they take the "Equal Protection Clause" of the 14th Amendment as protecting only African Americans but not women, gays, and lesbians, because the writers of the Amendment, after the Civil War, did not have these groups in mind (Chemerinsky, p. 87).

If one supported the equal rights of women, gays, and lesbians, then, of course, the 14th Amendment would now belong to a larger justification of everyone's equal rights.

I am not a member of the Catholic Church, but my doctoral studies focused on different theories of interpretation, so I do appreciate the multiple levels of Catholic analysis of scripture as a better alternative than a method that looks a lot like fundamental literalism.

There are various church interpretative practices, of course, that range from those who believe there is only one right interpretation of a text to those who imagine multiple interpretations. I come closer to the latter. The online newsletter *Aleteia* quotes the following from the Compendium of the Catechism of the Catholic Church:

> Sacred Scripture must be read and interpreted with the help of the Holy Spirit and under the guidance of the Magisterium of the Church according to three criteria: 1) it must be read with attention to the content and unity of the whole of scripture; 2) it must be read within the living tradition of the church; 3) it must be read with attention to the analogy of faith, that is, the inner harmony that exists among the truths of the faith themselves ((Philip Kosloski, 06/28/20).

If I were to translate this triad for the interpretation of the Constitution, I would say that the Constitution must be read and interpreted with a sense of civic solemnity, and in the company of those who have struggled for and protected its promise for justice, according to three criteria: it must be read with attention to its content and the greater whole to which it belongs, it must be read historically, and it must be read with the hopes and dreams of all the people.

If I were a Catholic, I wonder what it would take for me to abandon the multilayered Catholic tradition of textual interpretation and to submit to the narrow originalist's interpretation of the Constitution. I guess I would have to have different values, since it's one's values that lie behind one's interpretative theory.

The Sacred and the Solemn

Aug 2024

Both the sacred and the solemn elicit reverence—reverence for something other than ourselves. Both invite us to be reverent, but reverent toward very different appearances. The appearance of the sacred, whether in a temple or in nature, elicits a reverence toward the more-than-human. The solemn, on the other hand, resides in the all-too-human—in civic spaces such as court rooms and city council meetings.

We can feel reverence for different things such as our ancestors, the beauty of nature, and national cemeteries. I am not sure if these feelings are different from the feeling of reverence for a God. They are quite different, however, in terms of the language we use, the stories we tell, and their consequences.

My worry today is that groups like the Christian nationalists are violating significant "solemn occasions" with their "sacred agenda." To understand my worry, we must start with Donald Trump's pattern of turning solemn occasions into self-performances, such as riding the escalator to announce his candidacy for president. Instead of showing reverence for serious events, he plays with them. In a sense, he has banished the feeling of civic solemnity, at least for his followers, especially Christian nationalists.

Almost by definition, Christian nationalists overlook the solemnity of public events—from court proceedings to oath taking—because they see events from their view of God's providence. For them, all seriousness belongs to God. Democratic procedures, on the other hand, rest on the reverence for human dignity as it is manifested in courts of justice and other public proceedings.

It seems important to make a distinction between naïve and critical reverence. U.S. laws have sanctioned everything from slavery to genocide. A critical stance does not erase the legal order but rather seeks to improve it. The history of people who have protested unjust laws as well as of those who have protected the rule of law creates the context for our responsibility to maintain a critical feeling of solemnity toward "solemn occasions" in civic spaces.

No better way to practice this critical solemnity than thinking about the act of taking a public oath of office. I have an image of an oath-taker standing with one hand raised and the other hand on the Bible. Is this a solemn occasion or a sacred one? The ceremony uses the Bible (a sacred text) in administering the oath, but the oath is a promise to fulfill the duties of the office, not to obey a God. It is a serious occasion but not a sacred one. It is, in other words, a solemn occasion.

Solemn occasions might seem all-too-human. They rest on our best efforts to protect and to provide for each other. They link us to such values as freedom, justice, and community. They provide occasions to be serious about our life together and the challenges we all face.

Christian nationalists, it seems to me, destroy the solemnity of civic life by dismissing the all-too-human and pushing their religious ideology into the civic realm. Instead of taking our efforts to live together seriously, they ignore them and preach their sacred alternative.

True believers, after all, do not see themselves as subject to processes of argument and persuasion. At the same time, their beliefs may remind us that humility makes us human. We are not gods, but neither are we without dignity and honor. Our words and actions can create occasions that deserve a solemn response—a response that not only reminds us of what we have achieved but also what we should protect.

Care for Civilians

The Climate of Justice and the Protection of Civilians

Feb 2020

As you would imagine, in a climate of justice civilians are protected; protected by citizens who enforce the rule of law. When one considers the civilians killed in our wars—from the Indian wars to the Middle East wars—our social climate, for the most part, has been anything but just. In fact, our own legal tradition has been much more about the protection of property (land or enslaved people) than about the protection of civilians.

This does not mean that the military has never been used to protect civilians. During the period of Reconstruction after the Civil War, federal troops protected black civilians in the South from white racists. Federal troops were also used to protect people marching for civil rights in the 1950s and 1960s. Overall, however, our military has killed millions of civilians from the massacre of Sandy Creek to the civilians killed in Vietnam.

After World War II, the International Committee of the Red Cross wrote the Geneva Conventions for the protection of civilians. It made a distinction between combatants and civilians and stated that nations must limit the dangers for civilians in time of war. Most nations have signed on to this international humanitarian law. For the first time, the protection of civilians has a legal foundation that could serve as leverage for moving from a climate of injustice to a climate of justice.

Trump's policies toward immigrants, and especially his policy of separating children from their parents at our border, not only violates the rights of civilians, but also reinforces the climate of injustice.

So, who counts as a civilian or a citizen? I think the notions of civilian and citizen belong to the realm of the civic, not the social. I propose that we understand such social categories as privileged and vulnerable and translate them into civic terms of civilian and citizen. The civic sphere, in other words, is composed of civilians who are vulnerable and rely on the enforcement of the rule of law and citizens who have the resources and a responsibility to listen to civilians and to ensure that their rights are protected.

Most cities today have 'Civilian Review Boards" that illustrate this civic interaction between civilians who approach the Board requesting protection, and citizens who sit on the Board and have the ability-to-respond. When these meetings repair broken relationships, develop mutual trust, protect our habitat and develop policies that change unequal social structures, then we can witness the creation of a climate of justice.

Thinking like a Civilian

Feb 2021

All of us are civilians most of the time, but many of us rarely think like one. If we are to save the planet, we had better get on board. Warriors and soldiers will not get us where we need to go.

In researching and reflecting on what we need to do to protect the planet, I have concluded that we need to have some capacity to step into the shoes of civilians and see our society from their perspective. Protecting civilians and protecting the planet belong together—you cannot have one without the other.

During the demonstrations in Ferguson, Missouri, a black teenager told a news reporter; "The police treat us as suspects, rather than as civilians." Black Lives Matter can be seen as a protest against the violation of the civilian rights to protection and provision.

White men can also be civilians, but the challenge for us would be to accept that we cannot protect ourselves and must rely on the enforcement of law. That would mean the end of civilian armies, an acceptance of one's vulnerability, and an active engagement in promoting the rule of law. Sounds somewhat un-American.

On the other hand, the pandemic exposed everyone as vulnerable and as dependent on government agencies. Public health focuses on the health of the public and our public will not be healthy until the most vulnerable are protected. It doesn't take a genius to figure that out.

In a social climate of injustice, those with resources will exclude those without resources from the public realm. "They don't matter". In a social climate of justice, those with resources would provide protection and provisions for others.

The Civilian's Condition

Feb 2022

I learned about the significance of civilians in thinking about creating a climate of justice. The reason is not all that complicated: a climate of injustice was created by the enslavement, massacre, lynching, and the terrorizing of civilians. I doubt if we can create a climate of justice without them.

How does someone become a civilian? One's status as a civilian does not depend on class, race, gender, education, or other social distinctions. Part of the power of the notion of a civilian is that, strictly speaking, it is not a social category, but a civic one. I think that will become clear when we get to its broadest meaning. Let's start, however, with the term's most common location and then explore other locations with similar conditions.

Civilians in the World of War

Civilians are non-combatants. They are not in the fight, so to speak. At the same time, combatants are not civilians. There is nothing civil about killing others, even enemies, when your commander orders it. Soldiers are governed by a military code of conduct rather than any civil code. We may have a civilian government rather than a military dictatorship, but when our Presidents take on the role of "Commander-in-Chief," their commands are military, not civil.

Even though "civilians" have been seen as non-combatants in war, they have not been seen as non-targets. Just the opposite. As Roxanne Dunbar Ortiz has documented in her book *An Indigenous People's History of the United States,* the killing of civilians—from Wounded Knee to Iraq—has been part of our military's strategy. In the world of war, we can say that the conditions of civilians are that they are vulnerable, cannot protect themselves, and should be protected by the rule of law. These conditions occur not only in war, but also in times of economic despair.

Civilians in the World of Economic Despair

Perhaps the most famous non-military case of civilian protection was the Great Depression of the 1930s, when the "Civilian Conservation Corps" was created for unemployed men ages 17 to 28. These men (this was the 1930's) and their families were vulnerable, like civilians in the world of war, and they could not protect themselves and their families from hunger and depression. The government provided them protection through various programs that gave them paid work, which not only helped them, but also the country. Whereas the Geneva Conventions for the protection of civilians limited military aggression toward non-combatants—do not do harm—the Civilian Conversation Corps provided resources to vulnerable people—do some good. It expanded the implied civil rights of civilians to include not only the right to protection, but also the right to provision.

We can recognize civilians today in different social worlds—from public health care to urban environments—who are vulnerable, cannot protect themselves, and rely on the rule of law. Given this definition of the conditions of civilians, it's not that difficult to locate them in both our colonial past and our environmental future.

Civilians in Our Colonial Past

Our "success" as a colonial, settler nation depended on the appropriation of Indigenous people's land, which not only destroyed Indigenous communities, but also replaced the Indigenous people's sacred relationship with the Earth with a commercial relationship. The Earth became a thing to exploit rather than a living provider to honor. The Earth, in a sense, lost its protectors. The mountains, streams, forests, plains became as vulnerable to exploitation as the people who had protected them. In a sense, the Earth itself has suffered from the climate of injustice that has allowed so much misery for generations of civilians. To switch to a climate of justice, we would need to apply the laws that limit aggression in the world of war to the world of the natural environment. This is especially true when we turn to civilians in our environmental future.

Civilians in our Environmental Future

In terms of our planet's future, our children and grandchildren face the same condition as civilians: they are vulnerable, unable to protect themselves, and rely on the rule of law. We could also say, they rely on our civilian government to develop and implement policies that protect the Earth from destruction. They rely on us, in other words, to allow their claims for protection to create a civic space that is not subservient to military commercial, or technological interests, but is subservient to the foundation for democracy: a climate of justice.

Jeremiah in Ukraine

Mar 2022

Jeremiah has been my favorite prophet since my graduate days at Union Theological Seminary. I think I was influenced more by Abraham J. Heschel's lectures about Jeremiah than by the Book in the Bible. Several months ago, we visited Michelangelo's Sistine Chapel Exhibition at St. Mary's Cathedral in San Francisco, which included a photo of Michelangelo's Jeremiah.

The killing and suffering of civilians in Ukraine led me to imagine Jeremiah in Ukraine. What might we learn by imagining this prophet who lived in the seventh century BC as our contemporary? After reading the Book of Jeremiah again, as well as Heschel's book on the prophets, my assignment was not as easy as I had thought.

In *A Climate of Justice*, I engaged in a theological inquiry about the empowerment of civilians and I argued that the study of the gods can be understood as a study of power. Jeremiah appears to interpret this "power" in a particular way.

Heschel writes about the prophets, "The preoccupation with justice, the passion with which the prophets condemn injustice, is rooted in the sympathy with divine pathos." Jeremiah's prophecy of the demise of the Southern Kingdom or Judah by the Babylonians, in other words, was not some abstract prediction, but rather an expression of a caring and emotional God. This is the quality I see in Michelangelo's painting of Jeremiah.

> My soul will weep in secret for your pride
> My eyes will weep bitterly and run down with tears
> Because the Lord's flock has been taken captive.
>
> Jeremiah 13: 15-117

If that were the whole of Jeremiah's prophecy, I would not have had such a problem in imagining him in Ukraine. Another part of Jeremiah's message, however, is not so easy. Jeremiah focuses on "the

63

Lord's flock," as he says above. His focus is not on the empirical ambitions of the Assyrians, Babylonians, or Egyptians, who were the major political forces then, but on the Hebrews. If we were to simply apply what Jeremiah said to the tribes of Israel to the Ukrainian civilians, we would probably be accused of "blaming the victim."

It seems to me the best way out of this conundrum is to separate the pathos from the logos: the emotions from the argument. The Ukrainian civilians are not to blame for their plight. That does not mean that Jeremiah could not be there for them. He could even help us take in the emotional meaning of what is happening to all of us in our time.

When we witness the bombing of hospitals and maternity wards, our "pathos" of sorrow, grief, anger and rage is not lightened by some power above us, but rather deepened by the power among us.

Ukrainian Resistance and American Memories

Mar 2022

What does watching the pain and resistance of Ukrainian civilians trigger for you? What do you remember? American memory, of course, is complex and complicated, but in this case, Putin's war surely triggers different memories for different Americans

Ukrainian civilians say to us that they are not fleeing, because Ukraine is their home, their land. This is an indigenous argument, not available to those of us whose ancestors were colonists and settlers, but clearly available to Native Americans, who viewed the land as sacred.

The Westward expansion on other people's land took off following the War of Independence. The Treaty of 1763 between the British and the French prevented colonists from moving westward beyond their colonial settlements and recognized the land between their settlements and the Mississippi river as 'Indian Territory." One result of the American Revolution, if not one of the causes, was to open this land to speculators and settlers.

The successful Haitian revolution against Napoleon's army at the turn of the 19ᵗʰ century led Napoleon to sell what became known as the "Louisiana Purchase" in 1803, opening the land from the Mississippi river to the border of 'New Mexico." The Mexican war of 1846-1848 completed our expansion "from sea to shining sea."

Westward expansion also included the "Trail of Tears" from 1830 to 1850, the massacres of Sand Creek and Wounded Knee, and the displacement of many of the 500 tribes that inhabited the territory. Although I don't know, I could imagine that American Indians have the experience to know what it's like to be Ukrainian.

Those who attended a school like mine know something about American history, but we learned about it as settlers, not as natives. Our white memory, in other words, makes our past heroes look much more like Putin than like Zelensky. So, what do we do?

One option, of course, is to forget. Not to remember. Some Republican lawmakers have taken this option. "Let's ban from school whatever makes our white children uncomfortable." The other option is not simply the contrary. It's more complicated. We are not Putin, but we have been. We have practiced genocide. We have killed civilians. If we are Americans, we must remember this. But we are more than our memory. The second option is to say that we have committed crimes against humanity. We know the suffering our nation has caused, and we will never do it again. We could say that instead of bringing suffering to others, we will protect them. We are "recovering imperialists."

If truth be told, settler communities do not have the grounding relationship to the Earth that Indigenous communities have, but we can learn from them. Frankly, I don't know how we will get out of this mess, but it seems like a good idea to not block out American memories

Civilians after October 7

Oct 2023

Since the events of October, there's a lot of talk about the protection of civilians even as they are being killed by the thousands. President Biden traveled to the Middle East with the message that the Israeli military should not make the mistake we did after 9/11. What was the mistake? The attack on the people of Afghanistan and Iraq. Remember President Bush's "shock and awe" campaign?

It appears that Israel failed to protect its civilians. So many were left without protection from evil. What are we to make of that? Does it remind us of how we as a nation have often failed to protect our civilians, especially those subject to the terror of white supremacy?

Living in a post-October 7th war, the question now is who will protect Israeli and Palestinian civilians. Does Hamas aim to protect civilians or to use them? Perhaps Hamas believes that their fight for freedom is more important than the protection of Palestinian civilians. Civilians, from this perspective, become instruments of war, which is a clear violation of international humanitarian law.

Moral progress is a tricky business. We have stopped lynching in the United States. We have even called our "shock and awe" program a mistake. Many people today recognize both vulnerable Israelis and Palestinians as civilians. Despite all their differences, in this regard they are the same.

Not protecting civilians is not just a "mistake," it is a violation of international law as well as a debasement of our human responses to the horrors of war. One could use the double-effect theory to evaluate the morality of war. It held that if the impact of the harm you do is greater than the good you intend, then you should not do it. That should be enough to stop the bombing of Gaza. If we add the obligation to protect civilians, it must be stopped.

Overcome National Amnesia

If Truth Be Told

Sept 2022

If truth be told, we would eat a slice of humble pie, walk softly on the Earth, and give thanks for its gifts.

If truth be told, our zip code tells us more about our life chances than our DNA

If truth be told, we don't breathe the air, the air breathes us.

If truth be told, the Earth does not belong to anyone, we all belong to it.

If truth be told, it will come from the stories of vulnerable groups.

If truth be told, our nation does not have a soul. Maybe individuals do, settler nations do not.

It was not a "soul" that has held our nation together, but rather the white compromises that disavowed crimes against humanity and created a climate of injustice that has never been repaired.

If truth be told, rescuing the middle class will not rescue the planet.

If truth be told, the change we need will require the organization of both people and technology.

If truth be told, the climate crisis will change social relations. The question is whether we have the gumption to push the change toward a climate of justice.

If truth be told, any climate proposal that does not limit consumption is a fool's errand.

If truth be told, democracy without the rule of law leaves the most vulnerable exposed to harm.

If truth be told, single-mindedness disavows social relationships.

If truth be told, it's very difficult to change our beliefs. False beliefs make sense to us, or we would have already changed them.

If truth be told, truth usually doesn't win over safety.

If truth be told, democracy depends on caring citizens who listen to the claims of vulnerable civilians.

America's Soul and The Climate of Injustice

Feb 2023

As I wrote some time ago, the idea of an American soul does more harm than good in our quest to understand ourselves. I had hoped that Joe Biden would move on, but he continues to use the term on the campaign trail. When Joe Biden spoke of saving "America's soul" on the campaign trail, I hoped it was a temporary lapse, but it seems I was wrong. He said it again in his State of the Union address. Nation-states do not have souls. Neither do empires. It's a pretty wacky idea.

Biden got the idea from Jon Meacham's book, *The Soul of America: The Battle for our Better Angels* (2018).

> What is the American soul? The dominant feature of that soul—the air we breathe or to shift the metaphor the controlling vision–is a belief in the proposition, as Jefferson put it in the Declaration, that all men are created equal. It is therefore incumbent on us, from generation to generation, to create a sphere in which we can live, live freely, and pursue happiness to the best of our abilities. We cannot guarantee equal outcomes, but we must do all we can to ensure equal opportunities (8).

Well, it certainly stretches the imagination to believe that Jefferson ever breathed the breath that all men—let alone women—are created equal. Jefferson was the master of over 200 enslaved persons at Monticello. He was a settler on indigenous land. He was the father of the children of enslaved Black women. Could he breathe or would he more likely choke on the idea of human equality?

When my son and I visited Monticello a few years ago, we took the Sally Hemings tour. If there was something like a soul there, it was Black, not white. If we were to draw a map of the slave labor camps, also called plantations, before the Civil War, Monticello would be on the map.

So, it was somewhat of a surprise when I read the Black woman theologian Kelly Brown Douglas's book, *Resurrection Hope: A Future Where Black Lives Matter* (2021). There are a lot of good things about this book, especially her analysis of white supremacy as a "white gaze," and how she faces the difficultly of restructuring our social worlds. I do not claim that I have freed myself from this gaze, but I question her apparent agreement with the idea of America's soul.

> Jefferson, considered the "father" of America's democracy, was the principal architect of the

Declaration of Independence. As such, he projected
a vision of the nation's soul. "We hold these truths to
be self-evident," Jefferson wrote, "that that all men are
created equal, that they are endowed by their Creator
with certain inalienable rights, that among these are
Life, Liberty and the pursuit of Happiness." To be sure,
despite this vision, the echoes of his Anglo-Saxon/
white chauvinism shone through the Declaration as
Jefferson referred to Native Americans as "the merciless
Indian Savages, whose known rule of warfare, is an
indistinguishable destruction of all ages, sexes, and
conditions." Still the very enumeration of inalienable
rights indicates a vision that transcends the "raced"
assumptions behind the Declaration itself (32-33).

It isn't clear to me how a vision and an assumption could be so
contrary, but that's not the big problem. The big problem here is that
"soul" does not belong to a vision or an assumption. It belongs to a
community and a good soul would never belong to a community of
the master class.

The declaration of inalienable rights may not have soul, but it is
not nothing. Martin Luther King Jr. called it a "promissory note."
That seems right. Especially when we add the "promise" of the 14th
Amendment. If that's how we see it, and if broken promises harm all
of us, then we should be eternally grateful for those citizens who invite
us to repair them.

Let's take a step back. People say things and people do things—
words and deeds—and they always do them in a context that is either
maintained or changed by what they say and do. The social context in
1776 was established by the 150 years of creating prosperity through
enslaved labor and stolen land. As you probably know, the "1619
Project" tells us a lot about this context. I would add to that story
the story of white compromises that were made to protect American
prosperity. These white compromises silenced the voices that called

on us to keep our promises to ourselves and to others. The white compromises also maintained a social climate of injustice.

Our climate of injustice exists as a social world, a context, in which our everyday conversations either maintain or change it. What we say and do makes a difference. It makes a difference if we say that our "nation" began as a slave holding/settler colony, or we say it has a soul. If we want to create the conditions for dealing with our climate crisis, I think we had better stick with the truth.

The Trouble with Christian Nationalism

July 2023

What's troubling about Christian nationalism is not only its arrogance, but also its withdrawal from reality. At least that seems to be the conclusion of Pamela Cooper-White. She admits in her book, *The Psychology of Christian Nationalism*, that even though she tried to resist the notion of "two Americas," her research led her to change her mind (p.27). She is not alone in concluding that unity is not only impossible, but also disrespectful of the truth.

Cooper-White relies on the extensive research by Andrew Whitehead and Samuel Perry on Christian Nationalism, whose work she quotes in her book:

> It [Christian Nationalism] idolizes relations marked by clear (metaphorical or physical) boundaries and hierarchies both in the private and public realms. It baptizes authoritarian rule. It justifies the preservation of order with religious violence, whether that be carried out by police against deserving (minority) criminals, by border agents against presumptively dangerous (minority) immigrants, or by citizen "good guys" with guns against rampaging "bad guys" with guns. And it glorifies the patriarchal, heterosexual family as not

only God's biblical standard, but the cornerstone of all
thriving civilizations (p. 13).

We do live in different worlds, or what could be called different social
microclimates. The Bay Area has its "weather microclimate" as well as
its "social microclimates," as does Redding or Orange County. What
we should not forget, however, is that all these social microclimates
exist in a larger social context that has its origin in the Atlantic trade
of people and land, which has never been adequately corrected. This
larger social climate belongs to multiple social trends swinging back
and forth between exposing our legacy of injustices and denying them.
Although the white Christian mythology of domination—domination
of land and people—has been exposed as a violation of human dignity
and the Earth's integrity (see Kimmerer's book, *Braiding Sweetgrass),*
it continues to hold sway among Christian nationalists. So, how should
we deal with this?

We could start by deciding on an interpretation of the connection
between the social climate of injustice and the social climate of justice.
Do they exist side by side in two separate social worlds, or does one
follow the other, or is one the context for the other?

One could propose that the social climates of injustice and justice
exist side by side as the free and slave states did before the Civil
War. Until the war, and after Reconstruction, these two sides were
held together through political compromises for the sake of American
prosperity.

It's tempting to apply the more classical framework of fall from
grace and then redemption, but this framework doesn't fit our history.
We never had a period of grace. Virginia began as a slave colony.
We started with a climate of injustice. The Virginia plantations, even
Jefferson's Monticello, existed in a climate of injustice, as did the city
of Philadelphia. This social climate has never been adequately changed.

The third option is that our separate social microclimates—
our different worlds—exist in a larger social climate—a climate of
injustice. The trouble with Christian nationalism is that they take their

story not as one story among others in our larger social context, but rather as the whole story.

One may assume that true believers love the Christian nationalist's story. Maybe Cooper-White is right. It's a waste of time to try to get them to include the experiences of others in their story. It's not a waste of time, however, and we may not have a lot of time, to change the trajectories of our context from injustice to justice. We should not let the roaring of Christian nationalists distract us from the work that requires our attention.

Considering "America"

Apr 2024

Is the United States *in* or *of* America? Maybe a strange question, but perhaps one that can shed some light on our climate of injustice that needs correction. Isn't it obvious that "America" existed before the United States? Does the notion of "United States of America" obscure or reveal this fact?

So, what is the meaning of "of" in the phrase "United States of America? *The American Heritage Dictionary of the English Language* offers 21 options from "belonging to" like the "rungs on a ladder" to "coming-from," like "men of the north." None of the options can tell us for certain what Thomas Jefferson meant when he coined the phrase. (Before Jefferson, we had "united colonies," not "united colonies of America.").

It is a bit strange that we don't say "Mexico of America" or even "Israel of Palestine" but do say "United States of America." If you ask where Mexico is, the answer is "in Mesoamerica." And where is Israel? In Palestine. And the United States? Isn't it in America?

Do you know why America is beautiful, but the United States is not? And what is beautiful about America? Is it the land, the scenery, the landscape, the things-worthwhile-seeing? Is it the land with or without people?

In fact, the land of America was populated with over 500 communities before European settlers arrived. When our government was formed after the War of Independence, it was a nation controlled by European immigrants who had taken land and were intent on taking more of it from Native Americans.

Wouldn't it make sense to say that only Indigenous people are "of America"? The notion of "United States of America" not only erases their existence from white people's consciousness, but also makes our "taking of America" an action of white supremacy.

Some would say that we can use the notion "of" America however we want, because it is ours. We took America and we intend to keep it. "This land is your land, this land is my land, from California to the New York island." I used to sing this. Now I see that white supremacy is baked into this song, and it blinds us to the need to repair injustices.

Or to put it another way: America is only beautiful when it manifests the inclusion of indigenous communities who are truly "of America."

The Principle of Coherence and Conflicting Memories

Mar 2024

In a liberal household and even in a liberal society, we tend to let each other keep their memories, even when we disagree. Most of us do not appreciate someone telling us that our memories are wrong. In some cases, however, it's impossible that all the different views are true. So how can we tell? I think we can use the principle of coherence to help us decide.

The principle of coherence states that if A cannot be understood without B, then B cannot be understood without A. Here is an example of the principle:

> Just as you cannot understand black America without understanding white America, you cannot understand white America without understanding black America.

Or, what about this version:

> Just as you cannot understand Africa without understanding Europe, you cannot understand Europe without understanding Africa.

The first part of these statements makes sense. Does the second part? I think it does. Doesn't the European/African version make just as much sense as the black/white American version? Isn't it true that if you tell the story of Europe without any word about Africa, you have told the same half-truth as you would when telling the story of white America without any inclusion of black America?

In the previous post I analyzed the different meanings of the term, "America" as in "Native Americans or United States of America." In a sense, I had the notion of coherence in the back of my mind, even though I didn't say it. "If you cannot understand Native Americans without understanding "United States of America," then you cannot understand "United States of America" without understanding "Native Americans."

Using coherence to test our memories requires that we examine the complete historical context of our memories and then bring to our awareness the aspects of the context that we had previously ignored or dismissed. If we were to do this with our nation's history, I don't see how we can avoid the fact that our nation began in a climate of injustice.

This does not mean, of course, that we tell only the stories of enslavement and genocide; that would also be incoherent. We also remember the stories of the establishment of a democratic government that has been expanded from its original restrictions. In fact, if we remember the whole story, we will acknowledge our nation's climate of injustice, see possibilities for repairing these injustices, and move together toward a climate of justice.

Our Domestic Imperial Climate

May 2024

Of the many barriers to a climate of justice, few appear as difficult to overcome as the contempt for the rule of law that we are currently witnessing, which creates a climate of presidential imperialism. In a sense, of course, every US president is an imperial president, because the United States is an empire, beginning with the expansion of the United States into Indian Territory. Today, however, the empire's vibe is striking our democracy.

As Professor of Law at NYU Maggie Blackhawk documents in her essay, "The Constitution of American Colonialism" (Harvard Law Review, Nov. 2023), the laws of empire (or colonialism) existed as an external "constitution" separate from the "internal Constitution of the Bill or Rights and Equal Protection under the Law."

This external constitution consisted of such laws as the "doctrine of discovery" whereby one could colonialize any land that was "vacant" (Indigenous people do not count in the "discovery" of the Americas) and the right of civilized nations to dominate "uncivilized territories" (just in case Indigenous tribes were recognized). Maggie Blackhawk writes:

> Colonialism is commonly assumed to be antithetical to the constitution of the United States. It is, in many ways, constitutionalism's opposite. It is fundamental law that is dedicated to building and maintaining an empire. Its function is not to set and preserve borders but to expand them and to govern fragmented jurisdictions. The fundamental law of colonialism rejects equality for hierarchy. Colonialism builds power and infrastructure to allow the center to exert force over and govern others. . .. The realities of far-flung unilateral governance over nonconsenting "foreign" peoples, lands, and governments require a distinctive

set of fundamental values—hierarchy, a strong military,
a robust bureaucracy, and unrestrained power (p. 23)

Are not these the values of Trump followers? It does seem surprising that so many evangelical Christians appear to relish the imperial climate created at Trump's rallies. They seem to have forgotten that Jesus of Nazareth resisted rather than relished the Roman Empire. True, democracy was not an option in first century Palestine, and Jesus never had a chance to support a civic sphere. We have that option today and if we are not careful, we may lose it.

It's true that President Biden also occupies the imperial office, and for the most part, continues the colonial/imperial United States tradition. Still, he does not wear the emperor's clothes. He is not hollow enough inside to need them. He also does not allow external imperial values to override his domestic constitutional obligations, which cannot be said of Trump.

What's the Problem?

Nov 2024

Some say that the problem is Trump. He is to blame for our situation. Many, it seems, see him as the solution to the problem. That's why they voted for him. What problem they had in mind is not that easy to discern, but we can assume they voted for Trump because they thought it was the right thing to do, considering the world they think they live in. The problem could be, from this perspective, the world that Trump voters think they live in.

Two worlds that we sometimes separate and other times unite are the worlds of the economy or capitalism and the world of white male supremacy or cultural patriarchy. The two together comprise significant parts of the larger social world in which we live.

These two worlds have been present since the founding of our nation, The two key aspects of capitalism—extraction of value and domination—plus greed, coupled with the European settler's protection of their whiteness and their assumed status as a God-given superiority over others, created a climate of injustice that has never been corrected.

The two worlds share the drive of domination: domination of the planet, of women, of "others." Can you image a more perfect example of domination than Donald Trump? Kamala Harris, in my view, exemplified a different social climate. It is a view of the world that is more caring, more nurturing, and yes, more just. It looked like we were going to take a step forward, and instead we slide backwards. Time will tell how far before we step forward again.

Repair Social Damage

Are Reparations Necessary?

Sept 2020

If reparations are necessary, then it means that there is no other way to transform the current assault on our social and natural fabric into a livable and viable future. Reparations, in other words, have the capacity to repair our relationships with each other and with the Earth.

Whether that is true or not depends, in part, on our assumptions about the nature of social relations. I used to ask my students to make a list of terms that would define them. The list usually contained two types of terms: individual terms like honest and hard-working, and relational terms like sister and student. Male students and westerners tended to have more individual terms, and female students and non-westerners had more relational terms, as you might expect. In the discussion, everyone recognized they had "social relations," although some gave them more weight than others.

The peculiar nature of social relations is that the character of the relationship defines individuals rather than the character of the individuals defining the relationship. You may see yourself as honest regardless of others, but you cannot see yourself as a sister or a student by yourself. The kind of sister or student you are depends mostly on the social climate of your family and school.

Another characteristic of social relations is that they exist in history: they have a past history and a future history. Their "future history" is just a continuation of past patterns and expectations into the future. We live in history and if we don't change it, we repeat it. Conflictual social relationships, for example, have a theme or mythology that reinforces linguistic and behavioral patterns that carry its participants into the future until they decide to change its direction.

The linguistic and behavioral patterns in which we live not only shape our perceptions and expectations of ourselves and others, but also of the Earth. We generally see it as "land," as property, as an investment, and a source of entertainment and well-being. It is a thing, sometimes a beautiful thing, there for us. Instead of seeing ourselves as part of the larger whole, we see ourselves apart from it, just like we see ourselves apart from social relations rather than embedded in them.

Even though these social relationships largely define us, we also have the capacity, somewhat limited of course, to change them. I suppose most of us have had experiences of repairing broken personal relationships. What about social relations between different groups; like relations between men and women, or rich and poor, or black and white? These groups are also largely created by the social relations between them, so if you change the relations, you change the groups. Some are probably amiable and some conflictual. Sometimes, the social relationships benefit some at the expense of others. These are unjust social relationships.

You may think that unjust social relations are not really a problem. What about: "Life is unfair: get used to it." Or perhaps a more abstract mantra: "It is what it is." Such pronouncements might be more persuasive if we believed that current social and environmental trends were heading in a positive direction.

The problem, of course, is that things cannot continue as they are going. Not only is the disruptive potential of social problems becoming more powerful, but our planet is also becoming less and less inhabitable. Hotter temperatures, spreading fires, stronger winds, greater floods, strengthened hurricanes, colder winters, longer droughts, fewer species, increased pollution, ravaged coastlines: who wants such trends to continue?

If we live in a social system built and maintained by unjust relations—some have privileges at the expense of others—and if those with privileges fear they will lose their privileges if the system changes, and if they also know that the system cannot continue as it is into the future, then the change must both calm our fears and redirect the current system. Let's return to the idea of the "historical future."

If you want to change the future, you have to change the past: you have to change history. For example, instead of telling the story about how sharecropping became a kind of debt slavery that benefited some at the expense of others, let's tell a story about how this unjust relationship between farm laborers and landowners or between renters and property owners, can and will be corrected. Such a "correction" changes both parties in the relationship; the privileged and the exploited. The exploited not only receive some compensation, but also recognition. The privileged can stop defending their "superiority," and in joint action with others, deflate the social world of white male arrogance and aggression that is devastating the planet.

As a critical member of the privileged group, does this calm our fears? Can we allow the transformation of the social relations that have allowed us to see ourselves as superior to others? Can we let go of our arrogance? What if we realized that arrogance pulls us away from our shared humanity instead of drawing us toward it? After all, others are not asking the privileged to be heroes, but merely humans, which is not a bad way to live on the Earth.

Some would argue that what is missing is a strong will. "We can achieve whatever we set our mind to." "Afterall, we are America." Let's be honest here and recognize that it's the strong will of European settlers to advance "American prosperity" that created our fundamentally fragmented America. We don't need heroes; we need repairmen/women.

The social world of white male arrogance by itself cannot recognize the limits of its powers or the limits of the planet. It feeds off the ideology of "unlimited possibilities," which prevents persons who are participating in this white male world from making the changes necessary for a viable future. The process of implementing reparations might give us a chance to distance ourselves from this social world and then to transform it.

I think the process of reparations had this impact with Germany after WWII. They paid Israel money, but Germans also changed their culture and became less authoritarian and more democratic. The process of repairing broken relationships changed them as much as it helped Israel.

Could reparations do something similar for us? What would happen if civilians (those who are vulnerable to the powerful) invited citizens (those of us who have resources to protect and provide) to join them in repairing our relationships, correcting violations of our shared humanity, and restoring the Earth as a habitat for everyone? A process of reparations may not be sufficient to do this, but it may be necessary.

What to Replace and What to Repair

Mar 2021

You can replace some things. Some you cannot. Sometimes, you can follow Buckminster Fuller's famous saying: "You never change things by fighting the existing reality. To change something, build a new model that makes the existing model obsolete." And sometimes you cannot.

If we were dealing with a broken window, we can replace it with a new one. That's not the case with the legacy of white supremacy and arrogance. In fact, white supremacy depends on denying its legacy. We cannot replace that legacy; we must repair it.

Buckminster Fuller was quite remarkable, but it seems fair to acknowledge that he belonged to a company of white men who wrote as though they were not part of a social world that owed its prosperity to the enslavement and displacement of millions.

One does need to imagine a future. We all do that. We also need to consider our location in the racial history of our social structures, and to imagine how to change those social structures so that our imagined future is possible. The future, in other words, comes to us from behind, and we cannot realize it until we turn around.

As I see it, the current course of American prosperity that relies on the exploitation of labor and the depletion of the planet must be redirected toward a sustainable future. This kind of structural change involves repairing the injuries that American prosperity has caused. Reparation is not just about being accountable to others, but also about resetting our future possibilities.

I know some things cannot be repaired and must be replaced. One could see European/Americans as people who chose to replace their home country rather than repair it. I assume that many of us would rank "the freedom to leave" high on any list of human rights. Still, the choice does not have to be between "love it or leave it." We can also work to change our social climate to a climate of justice, and that will require that we replace social amnesia with social awareness.

A Case for Reparations

July 2021

Paying people for unpaid labor seems like a no-brainer, except for the facts of the case. Then things get complicated. From the perspective of the Climate of Justice Project, the basic standard is clear: "Does a particular reparation policy promote a climate of justice?"

A climate of justice is about more than money. Money is the easy part. After seeing the government spend billions, or was it trillions, in the past year, we can assume that money is available whenever the government wants to create it. Money certainly is part of the picture, but we need to see the picture first.

Reparation involves a "repair," and what needs repair are the social relationships among us. Currently, the social relationships among people of privilege and people of color are unjust. One problem is that some of us have taken this climate of injustice as "normal," which easily makes any reparations for specific groups seem like discrimination—favoring one group over another—rather than changing an unjust situation to a more just one.

If all things were equal, of course, there would not be a reason for reparation. That's not the case, as study after study shows. If the inequalities were "natural," reparations would also have a hard time gaining acceptance. If the inequalities were intentional, on the other hand, then it's a different story. If they were intentional, then the inequalities are a crime: a crime against humanity.

Our settler ancestors intended the social worlds in which we live today, and these social worlds continue as a climate of injustice. This social climate of injustice blocks not only the repair of broken social relationships but also the repair and protection of the planet. All the debates about reparations are not only worthwhile but also necessary, if we want to pass on to all our children an inhabitable Earth.

Philanthropy vs Reparations

Dec 2021

One would hope that philanthropy could promote justice. After all, that's where the money is. According to Rob Reich, the Director of the Stanford Center on Philanthropy and Civil Society, the total capitalization of foundations in 2014 was more than $800 billion. On the other hand, as Julia Travers points out in her recent article in *Inside Philanthropy*, less than 2 percent of funding from our largest foundations targeted the black community in 2011.

Because foundations are tax-exempt, Reich estimates they cost the US government at least $50 billion in forgone federal tax revenue. That doesn't seem fair. Reich does not conclude in his book *Just Giving* (2018) that foundations are necessarily unjust, but rather that they can and should find more innovative solutions to social issues.

Supporting institutions that are addressing past injustices would seem to fit this prescription. The question is whether a philanthropic perspective can comprehend the meaning of reparations. There are differences. Differences in conceptualizing the problem, in defining the relationships, and in changing the context.

Conceptualizing the Problem

For the most part, the philanthropic perspective locates the problem with the receivers of the help. They need things. It may be things they deserve if they have been exploited or harmed, but the solution is largely to increase their resources.

Reparations focuses on repair. The repair involves making things right. What "making things right" means will depend on the negotiations among the parties involved.

Defining the Relationships

In the world of philanthropy, there are givers or donors and receivers. Donors take pride in their good deeds, as they should from their perspective. Still, the relationship tends to be feudalistic with subjects of the crown becoming patrons of their lords. True, some donors may try to empower others, but they seldom dis-empower themselves.

Reparations define the relationship between the participants very differently. No one has put their finger on the key character of reparations better than Ta-Nehisi Coates:

> Reparations beckon us to reject the intoxication of hubris and see America as it is— the work of fallible humans (*We Were Eight Years in Power*, 2017, p. 202).

Reparations, in other words, not only impacts those who have been harmed, but also the perpetrators, or more generally, the benefactors of racism. The issue here is white supremacy and arrogance. What's the opposite? White contrition? White humility? At least, reparations would mean that instead of inviting the vulnerable to apply for our assistance, we would listen for their invitation to join them in making a viable future for all of us.

Changing the Context

We live today in a context of injustice—a climate of injustice. No better evidence than the unequal distribution of Covid 19 vaccines. This distribution could be seen as an example of the philanthropic approach. The wealthy nations get their vaccines, and then donate vaccines to the rest.

Reparations aim to change the current context to a climate of justice. When the vulnerable invite us to protect them, they invite us to leave our superior status and to become one among others, living together on the Earth. I think we need this change in our social climate to save the Earth as a human habitat for all.

Reparations Benefit All of Us

May 2023

Some of the talk about reparations seems to assume that reparations will only benefit Black people, but unrepaired social injustices don't work like that. They hurt all of us.

The basic premise of my book *A Climate of Justice* is that until we repair the debilitating legacy of past injustices, we will not have the possibility of saving the planet. Our social climate of injustice, in other words, prevents us from joining together to handle the climate crisis. That premise makes a lot of sense if you have been paying attention.

Some of the proposals for addressing our climate crisis simply avoid the social context. Let's drive electric cars with rechanging stations on all our highways and roads. Let's extract carbon from the air and subsidize solar panels on homes and businesses. And so on, as though our social context didn't exist. We can send rockets to the moon while people are dying on the streets.

This is nothing new. What's new is that the social divisions are growing just as much as the climate crisis. When around 30 percent of our population follow a fascist leader, building windmills reminds one of Don Quixote.

The last thing white fascists want, of course, are government programs that address past injustices through reparations. I must admit that at least the Republican leadership seems to take note of policies and programs that aim at changing our social climate from a climate of injustice to a climate of justice. What they don't understand is that their defense of a climate of injustice prevents us from creating a public and civic context that would enable us to move toward a sustainable habitat for all of us.

We are making some progress: a few confederate monuments have been removed. Names have been changed. A few organizations, such as Georgetown University, have addressed the issue of reparations. At the same time, the resistance has grown. But the resistance, in a sense, may be a sign of progress.

Changing a social climate is tough, especially on the issue of race. Still, I think it is a necessary struggle not only for justice, but also for creating a habitat for everyone.

Change the Conversation

The Coronavirus and the Language of War

Mar 2020

In responding to the pandemic, the government has slipped into the language of war. Like other languages, it belongs to a system of thought that provides a framework for talking about a problem, how to solve it, and what "victory" looks like. Let's think about this for a minute.

There are other options than war talk. The civil rights movement, for example, was not framed as a "war against discrimination" or a "war against white supremacy." It was a movement seeking protection for people's civic rights. The movement certainly encountered hostile forces, and the federal government sent troops to protect demonstrators, but these troops were not fighting a war. They were protecting civilians.

In the language of war, there are two groups: combatants and civilians. Combatants fight each other and civilians suffer the consequences. This doesn't fit well with our situation where caregivers, not warriors, have the experience and courage to deal with our health crisis.

It's not that the language of war is unpopular. Gun sales have increased throughout the nation. Guns don't kill viruses; they kill people. The language of war easily ends up creating an enemy. The

President's calling the coronavirus a "Chinese virus" fits in this framework.

The language also divides us into winners and losers, which appears to define much of Trump's world. If one takes up this distinction, when would we know who wins or who loses? Here we see a potential dilemma: Do we win when the vulnerable are protected or do we win when American prosperity returns? Is this the way we want to frame the issue?

We have had social wars before such as the war on poverty or the war on drugs. They ended up disempowering groups rather than empowering them. What have we learned from these experiences?

Maybe if our language was grounded more in the language of care and nurture, we would have a better grasp of what a climate of justice would require. There is no shortage of caregivers who could promote such a climate. Let's make room for their voices.

It's not like war, it's like the New Deal

Mar 2020

In my last post, I argued that the language of war was inappropriate for talking about the coronavirus epidemic. When the Governor of New York tells us that ventilators are as necessary as missiles, what appeared inappropriate becomes a bit ridiculous. Considering not only the public health crisis, but also the economic crisis (and the environmental crisis), would not the language spoken during the Great Depression in the 1930s be a much better choice?

So, what were people talking about? Here's a list of their programs (from *The Living New Deal* web site).

Agricultural Adjustment Act

Armed Forces and National Defense Industries

Army Corps of Engineers

Art & Culture Projects of the Federal Emergency Relief Administration

Bankhead-Jones Farm Tenant Act

Banking Act

Bonneville Power Administration
Bureau of Public Roads
Bureau of Reclamation
Civil Aeronautics Act
Civil Works Administration
Civilian Conservation Corps
Communication Act
Emergency Banking Relief Act
Fair Labor Standards Act
Farm Credit Act
Federal Deposit Insurance Corporation
Federal Emergency Relief Act
Federal Emergency Relief Administration
Federal Parks Reorganization
Federal Project Number One
Federal Aert Project
Federal Security Agency
Federal Surplus Commodities Corporation
Federal Works Agency
Fish and Wildlife Conservation Act
Glass-Steagall Banking Act
Gold Reserve Act
Homeowners Loan Act
Indian Reorganization Act
National Housing Act
National Industrial Recovery Act
National Labor Relations Act (Wagner Act)
National Youth Administration
Post Office Department
Public Building Administration
Public Works Administration
Public Works of Art Project
Puerto Rico Reconstruction Administration
Repeal of Prohibition
Resettlement Administration

Robinson-Patman Act
Rural Electrification Act
Rural Electrification Administration
Section of Fine Arts
Securities Act
Social Security Act
Soil Conservation Act
Soil Conservation Service
Taylor Grazing Act
Tennessee Valley Administration
Travel Bureau
Treasury, Public Buildings Branch
Treasury Relief Art Project
Housing Act
Virgin Islands Company
Wagner-Peyser Act / U S Employment Service
Works Progress Administration.

This list of programs reveal a government that is not at war against some enemy, but rather a government that seeks to ensure that its people have the resources for their provision and protection.

Trump Voters vs. Public Health

April 2020

I can imagine that some Trump voters have rolled their eyes more than once when learning what they voted for when voting for Trump. The latest, and perhaps the deadliest, is their vote against public health. Some voters may not have intended this, but whatever their intention, that seems to be the consequence.

So, what is the meaning of public health? You could see it as a positive response to social sickness. By "social sickness" I don't mean being sick of social media, or what some might call a "sick society," but rather illnesses that occur because of our participation in various social worlds. From this perspective, the coronavirus appears as a social sickness and public health a government solution.

A brief history of the government's program in public health, could start with the story of the governmental response to sailors and disabled seaman in 1798 with the establishment of Marine hospitals. The scope of public health continued to expand with national quarantine and disinfection measures, as well as immunization programs. By the early 20th century, the government investigated such diseases as tuberculosis, hookworm, malaria, and leprosy, and it also looked at sanitation, water supplies, and sewage disposal. More recently, the Public Health Service has responded to the diseases of lung cancer, chronic bronchitis, AIDS, and to health issues after Katrina and other hurricanes.

The reason for focusing on social sickness is to give a context for public health. If someone doesn't recognize social reality—they may believe only individuals exist—as is the case for libertarians, then public health would limit itself to curing sick individuals, rather than preventing them from getting sick. I don't know if Trump has a contextual notion of the social in his conceptual framework.

A more important question is whether Trump has a notion of the public. Public health refers to the government—on various levels—engaged in preventing social sickness. Universal health care, of course, would aim to prevent social sickness by giving people access to health care. It makes more sense, given the language of social sickness and public health, to say that universal health care is not a social program, but a public program. Just as we have public schools and public parks, we also need a public health system to ensure a vibrant democracy.

When Trump cuts the funding for the Department of Health and Human Services, and even the Centers for Disease Control and Prevention, when he lowers the standards for carbon emissions, when he refuses to develop a national plan to address the coronavirus crisis, what conclusion can one draw other than he hates the public? Some of his voters probably do as well. My guess is that some do not. In any case, that is what they got.

The Public and the Social

May 2020

The epidemic continues to challenge our thinking and feelings about our understanding of ourselves. Sickness and death, of course, are always present; but they are not always public. They are not always so clearly defined as issues of public health.

One can see without question the social dimensions of the epidemic—its impact on the young and old, the responses of men and women, its danger for those who work at home and those who work in meat processing plants, hospitals, and eldercare homes. Public health certainly considers these social differences in its responses to the epidemic, and may treat different social groups differently, but none of them should be excluded from the public realm.

What has become thought-provoking is the meaning of our public realm. We have public schools, public parks, public beaches, public libraries, public housing, public works, public leaders, and of course, public health. Would not it have been wise to call social security "public security"? So, how does this realm fit in our interpretative frameworks?

One classical framework has three elements: the economy, government, and civil society. The public—funded and managed by local, regional, or national taxpayers and managed by elected or appointed public servants—clearly belongs to government, or what I would call civic government. (Our government has both civil and military functions, and today at least, public health belongs to civic government.) For-profit hospitals would belong to the economy and non-profit hospitals to civil society. Both belong to various social worlds as well. (Some people in civil society deny their social identity, but that doesn't make it disappear).

In the civic realm, social differences are recognized and mediated. In this realm, we are equal in terms of human dignity, and different in terms of social position and relations. As I see it, these differences can be generally understood as differences between those who are vulnerable and need protection and those who have resources to provide protection.

Public health programs could be understood as implementing "public security" by using citizens' resources to protect vulnerable civilians. Any one of us could be a civilian—that's the nature of epidemics—which means that we could then call upon citizens to protect us, and thereby, of course, also protect them.

As the epidemic has continued, social differences have become exaggerated and aggravated. I see the anti-government protestors at state capitals as continuing a tradition of the "Lost Cause" that confederates and Christian ministers developed after the Civil War. They took their defeat as a sign of their superior moral status to the federal government. The resentment underlying this perspective has been enflamed by Trump's rhetoric. While they may take up airtime, we should not let them divert our attention from securing public health and security for all.

When is it a Mistake to Agree to Disagree?

July 2020

Sometimes "we cannot just get along" because we don't see a deeper mutuality that underlies our conflict. And sometimes, we become so invested in our cause that a deeper mutuality is not available.

Take the issue of taking down confederate monuments. Is it a mistake to talk with people who oppose our views?

A basic premise of my book *The Ethical Process*, and even more explicitly in *Learning through Disagreement*, is that people with opposing views know something I do not know. Dealing with disagreement is a learning process. The books outline a process of exploring the different observations, values and assumptions of opposing views for the purpose of making the best decision possible given what everyone knows. (No one knows everything!)

Not a bad idea, but not always workable, especially in a context defined as a war between winners and losers. In fact, it's not so much the arguments we make, but rather the social worlds in which they are made, that determines whether learning—on both sides—is possible.

When should we agree to disagree? When accepting our differences honors personal dignity. People disagree about religious truths, for example, but forcing agreement has certainly caused much more harm than honoring differences—agreeing to disagree.

On the other hand, when agreeing to disagree supports a status-quo that protects white supremacy and dismisses long standing injuries, then it's a mistake to agree to disagree.

When the necessary "deeper mutuality" is not available because it has been torn apart by crimes against humanity, then these violations must be repaired before we can see what we might learn from each other.

Language matters: "Plantation" or "Slave Farm"?

Nov 2020

As you may have read, the voters of Rhode Island will decide on Tuesday whether to delete the word "plantation" from their state name: 'The State of Rhode Island and Providence Plantation."

A few years ago, we took a bus along the Mississippi river from New Orleans to the "Whitney Plantation." Their tour centered on the stories collected by the Federal Writers' Project during the Depression of enslaved people, some of whom had lived there. The tour began with each of us receiving a card with a photo of a child's statue and name. We put the string attached to the card around our neck before we entered a small chapel. Our host told us that our cards matched the statue of a child in the room; a child who was born into slavery before the Civil War. I went over to Albert Paterson's statue, and read what was written on the back of his card:

> I remember our plantation was sold twice befo' de war. It is sheriff's sale, de white peoples dey stand up on de porch an de black men an' women an' children stand on de ground, an' de man he shout, "How much

am I offered fo' plantation an' fine men and women?"
Somebody would say so many thousands...an' after
while one man buy it all.

The tour then took us to a wall with the names of the place's
enslaved people. They also had a cage used to "discipline" unruly
workers, and the slave quarters. The tour ended with a walk-through
the master's mansion. So, what should we call this place?

Have you been to Monticello, Thomas Jefferson's "what do you
call it?" Over 200 enslaved people lived there when Jefferson died.
He inherited over half of them from his wife's father, who raped (is
that the best word?) Sally Hemings' mother. Jefferson then "raped"
Sally Hemings when she was 16 and he was 47. Jefferson's wealth was
based on slave labor and the selling of enslaved people (is that the right
word?). It turns out that Monticello was much more than "Jefferson's
home."

Don't you think we could find a better name for those "farms"
whose produce was planted, raised, harvested, and packaged by
enslaved labor as well as those farms that were engaged in the breeding
of enslaved people. The term "concentration camps" might be an
option. The term was used at first to signify a "concentration" of
people in a restricted area, but today it refers to the Holocaust. Does
"plantation" have a similar meaning for you?

What about "enslavement farms"? They were agricultural
enterprises or farms. And enslaved people created their wealth. Not
bad, but the term seems to slight the horrors committed by the enslavers.

The people of Rhode Island are not thinking about replacing
"providence plantation" with "enslaver's farms." That may seem like a bit
much, at least for many. Still, maybe we should stop using the "P" word.

We can change our vocabulary. The city of Berkeley, for example,
now celebrates "Indigenous Peoples' Day" instead of "Columbus Day."
It all depends on the stories we tell, and, of course, the stories we have
been told. It may be that we cannot tell the truth until we find the words.

D.E.I. vs U.M.E.

June 2023

David French recently wrote in the *New York Times* that it would be a good idea to not use "D.E.I." anymore because it has been misused (1/15/2024). He suggests that an organization could still support "diversity, equity, and inclusion," without using such a controversial phrase.

People have said similar things about "anti-racism" and "Black Lives Matter" and even "global warming." Why use words or phrases that cause controversy? "Just do the right thing!" Well, it's not that simple. In most cases, if you cannot imagine a different world, I doubt if you will be able to create one. That doesn't mean that we will not make mistakes in implementing a vision, it just means that change involves choices.

It may seem like institutions have a choice of either affirming D.E.I. or not, but I don't think that's the correct way of formulating the alternatives. "Not" is not a choice. Institutions either affirm D.E.I, or they, at least implicitly, affirm something else. The decision not to do something keeps in place the status quo, which could also use a title. And what would be a good title for what many of us are used to? What about "U.M.E." for "Unity, Merit, and Exclusion"? Let's examine these alternatives.

Unity sounds like a good idea, but it needs a context. It's hard to deny the dis-unity of our historical context, and its legacy. In this sense, diversity is not an idea, but a fact. So, what do we do with this fact? Make calls for unity? Well, you can bend people's minds, but you cannot bend the facts. Another option is to make a distinction between social diversity and a shared humanity.

We share our humanity, but not the same social worlds. If we remember that diversity is a social category (for the most part), and not an essential human category, we could affirm both social diversity and human unity, or at least, as I argue in *A Climate of Justice*, we could create a civic sphere where citizens and civilians (from different social worlds) come together based on their shared humanity. If "unity" is understood correctly, in other words, it would facilitate diversity, rather than deny it.

Merit assumes that we have similar starting points, so to speak, and those who win get the prize. They may "win" through hard work, talent, or luck. In any case, what merit doesn't recognize is that "winners" never win alone. Winners exist in a social world of many "others" who also play their role in maintaining a social world. Whereas "merit" is blind to these others, equity not only sees their place and their contribution to the larger whole but also the relationships among the parts of the larger whole and then ensures that the relationships are fair or just.

If unity assumes that we are all the same, and merit assumes that significant differences are based on "hard work, talent, or luck," then it is inevitable that those who are "other" will be excluded. In this framework, the only explanation for differences is that some work harder, have more talent, or more luck than others.

The fact that some have more privileges than others never come to mind. Nor does the fact that some have been harmed more than others by the social traumas of American history. A commitment to unity prevents us from listening to the experiences of others. It also leads to a gross misunderstanding of how "merit" is distributed. Finally, it prevents us from fulfilling the promise of equal justice.

Just as unity and merit lead to exclusion, diversity and equity lead to inclusion. If we want inclusion (if we must have it for the sake of a climate of justice), then we must choose D.E.I. over U.M.E.

Digital and Human Languages

Dec 2023

When I imagine conversations that promote a climate of justice, I have assumed that the conversations would be in our "mother tongue"— the language that helped us become part of the world in which we live. For many of us, this world is changing dramatically through the development of a different language: the language of digital technologies.

Meghan O'Gieblyn's book *God Human Animal Machine* (2021) provides a good opportunity to explore this situation. The challenge is already in the book's title: four categories without any connection, not even commas. Not the way we usually talk with one another.

And then there is the sub-title: *Technology, Metaphor, and the Search for Meaning.* Now that I can relate to. The "search for meaning" was the title of a book by Victor Frankl, who wrote about his search for meaning in the Nazi concentration camp at Auschwitz. Quite a different search than O'Gieblyn's search in the world of digital information.

O'Gieblyn's book tells two stories. One is a very accessible account of the development of digital technology from Ray Kurzweil's 1999 book, *The Age of Spiritual Machines,* to our present experience with "bots." She tells this story from her perspective, of course, and yet she allows us to listen to the arguments of scientists and visionaries.

Readers learn about Kurzweil's "transhumanism," "emergentism," Bostrom's simulation hypothesis, panpsychism, and more. This story of the development of "digital language" can be seen as a "search for meaning" in the various utopias of artificial intelligence.

The book's second story touches on a few episodes in O'Gieblyn's development. She grew up in a fundamentalist Christian community that demanded total obedience to a god beyond human understanding. She left this "world," and after some time, joined the "world" of digital technology. She brought with her, however, the fundamentalist ideology of an omniscient god.

Throughout the book, she draws parallels between the god that demands obedience without understanding and "transhuman" machines that appear to make similar demands: to submit to their knowledge without understanding. I think she ultimately rebels against digital omniscience as she rebelled against her fundamentalist god. In both cases, O'Gieblyn rejects what I would call the language of domination and thereby leaves open the possibility for a more humane language. That possibility only comes to light fully in her acknowledgements at the end of the book. She writes: "And thank you most of all to Barrett, whose unfailing love has taught me, more than anything else has, what it means to be human."

This acknowledgement of the importance of human relationships aligns with my chapter "Our Humanity" in *A Climate of Justice*. After pointing out that humans belong to the biosphere, I present the neurobiological research of Antonio Damasio, who sees the "autobiographical self" as the capacity to witness ourselves as living in an environment; Daniel Siegel, who sees the self as fundamentally interpersonal; and Attachment Theory, which affirms our primal need to relate to others. There is no transcendent god here nor ruling algorithms, only the desire for connection and reciprocity.

I agree that we need to figure out how to live in the world of technology. Our suggestions will largely depend on our experiences of human relationships, and how we talk about them. I think O'Geiblyn is right to resist the domination of digital language as she resisted the god of fundamental Christianity. Still, there are other forms of Christianity than the fundamentalist kind; forms that see God as a suffering servant or an advocate for the poor, or even as a vulnerable child in Gaza and Israel. If your relationship to digital language is to be evaluated by your theology, God's love for the vulnerable may be a better measurement than God's transcendence.

Highlight the Context

Why we need Contextual Thinking

Aug 2020

Instead of saying "consider the source" when we hear something strange, we could also say "consider the context." While the first option takes us to the speaker's story, the second one takes us to their situation. In a way, it's the difference between a psychological and a sociological approach. Or, between an individualist and a systemic interpretation.

There are certainly white racist men, but there is also a white male social world—a context that allows white men. to get away with things. Non-whites and many women know this social world because they experience it as having expectations and perceptions that are different than theirs. Contextual thinking allows us to pay attention to these differences.

Contextual thinking sees persons as participating in a social world; a world that is created and maintained by communication patterns and ways of doing things. An obvious example would be a burial at a grave site. For most of us, it's clear what clothes to wear, what is said and not said, even how we touch and look at each other. Some attendees may rebel, and maybe for good reasons, but few would fail to know "where we are."

Another prime example is a session in a courthouse. I remember sitting in the back row with my classmates when I was in high school.

I guess I was messing around a bit, which I stopped immediately when the judge announced that talking was not allowed and if we continued, we need to leave. In such cases, the appropriate behavior was not based on character, but on the situation—the solemn context.

Knowing the context, of course, is not always that easy. We all learn about it as we grow up and as we enter new contexts. We usually watch and listen to see what is appropriate. It gets fairly complicated as we move from one context to another. In some cases, it's about fitting in, or being invited, or belonging. There are also cases where we resist conforming to the context because we feel unseen or are asked to be someone we are not. Perhaps what is most difficult is when you believe the context needs to be changed, but just as you did not create the context by yourself, it's probably impossible for you to change it.

You could just avoid it. Pretending things just are what they are, so to speak. A shining example of this approach is fundamentalist Christians who read the Bible as though it was not written in particular times and places, for particular purposes in response to particular audiences and so on. It's a shame that so many Christians know so little about the Bible's historical contexts. For me the historical context made the Bible more accessible than reading it as though it belonged to our world today.

Living in our pluralistic multi-cultural world today makes contextual thinking necessary and difficult. It may not seem necessary for those of us who are privileged to live in a world that benefits us at the expense of others. That's not a bad definition of privilege: taking advantage of how a context favors us without admitting it. There are cracks in this frame, however, such as the continuing destruction of the planet as our habitat and the pandemic.

It's not a bad idea to assume that most of us do the best we can, given our circumstances, or at least, most of us do what we think is right, given the world we think we live in. If that's the case, then it's the context that deserves our attention. Sometimes, it's easier to recognize the context of others than our own. That's especially true for those of us who count our accomplishments as things we did, as though our context didn't make a difference.

Expanding our Contextual Awareness

Feb 2022

The fact is that we always live in some historical context. The liberal tradition, for the most part, dismisses this fact, and focuses on individuals and on the future—the world of unlimited possibilities.

The social philosopher, Kenneth Burke, said that to fully understand any human action, you must know something about the actor, the action, the actor's purpose, when it happened and where it happened. (Who? What? Why? Where? When?) These questions are also called the "journalistic questions" because answering the questions is an efficient way to write a full report of any incident. Interestingly enough; 2 out of the 5 (where and when) refer to the social and environmental context.

In a sense, contextual awareness is a part of everyday life. When we meet at a "social gathering," for example, we usually follow the contextual expectations to avoid any uncomfortable exposure of both us and others. In such settings, "we" share the same context and ignore differences that would disrupt our polite conversations.

These "social gatherings," however, are contained in a larger context where the polite unity of the "we" splits into disunity. Instead of relations among equals, we see relations among unequals, relations among the arrogant and the vulnerable, relations among whites and people of color, relations among the perpetrators and victims of crimes against humanity.

What Viet Thanh Nguyen says in his book *Nothing Ever Dies: Vietnam and the Memory of War* about the difference between an ethnic box and its racial content could help us to identify this broader context of crimes against humanity

> We might say that the form of the box is ethnic, and its contents are racial. The ethnic is what America can assimilate, while the racial is what America cannot digest. In American mythology, one ethnic is the same,

eventually, as any other ethnic; the Irish, the Chinese, the Mexican, and, eventually, hopefully, the black, who remains at the outer edge as a defining limit and the colored line of ethnic hope in America. But the racial continues to roil and disturb the American dream, diverting the American way from its road of progress. If form is ethnic and content is racial, then the box one opens in the hopes of finding something savory may yet contain that strange thing, foreign by way of smell and sight, which refuses to be consumed so easily: slavery, exploitation, and expropriation, as well as poverty, starvation, and persecution (p. 99).

Some Americans will find this exposure of content much more unsavory than others. In fact, for some, such exposure may allow them to be seen and respected. Others, especially if they cannot distinguish their humanity from the inhumanity of the context, will rebel against the truth. They will understand the notion of a "climate of injustice," in other words, as an indictment of them as inhumane. Remember, we are not our context, but until we change the content, we live in it.

"We" have different relations with our context, in other words, and therefore different relations with each other. Expanding our social contextual awareness allows us to see how others see us, and for us to reflect on how we see ourselves. Contextual awareness can expand, in some cases, self-awareness.

Whether our social gathering is inside or outside, it occurs not only in a social context, but also in a natural or environmental context. This context also has a history and a legacy. Our nation was not only founded on slave labor, but also stolen land. Only with the arrival of European colonists and settlers, was the American Earth treated as a commodity, as a thing. The long history of treating the Earth as our dominion, rather than our shared habitat—to see ourselves apart from nature rather than a part of nature—has unbalanced our relationship with nature,

Expanding our contextual awareness could help us see ourselves from the perspective of the devastation of the natural world. The social and the natural context in other words, are not unrelated. As a leader in the field of environmental justice, Carl Anthony, said some time ago:

> The dehumanization required to enslave people rests upon the same arrogance that allows the dominators to use, abuse, and pollute Earth's living ecosystem. This dehumanization continues when the contributions of people of color are missing from the history of the modern world. Humanity cannot develop a radically new ecological conscience until we re-tell its story to include the various histories and perspectives of people of color. Attempting to solve the problem of ecosystem exploitation will never work without facing up to its companion—waste and human exploitation caused by racism (*The Earth, the City, and the Hidden Narrative of Race* 2017, p. 17-18)

The deconstruction of arrogance, especially systems of arrogance, is no easy assignment. The problem is that we continue to live in a context—a climate of injustice—that allows and sometimes awards arrogance. To change this context is to change American mythology.

The Context of Character

Feb 2023

Martin Luther King Jr. stated in his "I Have a Dream" speech that he hoped that one day his children would be judged not by the color of their skin, but by the content of their character.

Well, as we learned from the police killing in Memphis, it's not a character's content, but rather a character's context that makes the biggest difference.

Like most cases, the context has multiple layers. Tyre Nichols was a Black man. Can you imagine the behavior of the police officers if he had been white? Tyre was not seen, I assume, as a person who deserved respect, but as an object, a thing, that could be beaten. These five officers would probably not beat a person to death, not someone like their wives or children, but someone who in their context was made to seem worthless. First deny a person's dignity, then kill them.

Tyre Nichols did not create the context; the Memphis police culture did by their uniforms, their weapons, their patrol cars, their talk, their silence, and their assignments that gave them the character of impunity. This created a stage for a horror show.

My guess is that the family members and friends of some of these officers were shocked by their loved one's behavior. They must have looked "out of character." And maybe they were out of character or maybe their character reflected their context. As they say, "Most people do what they think is right considering the world they think they live in."

The Climate of Justice Project is about context. It places a stronger emphasis on the social than on the individual. I know we need to balance the two, but we will never understand police killers, or political extremists, or religious fanatics until we develop a strong sense of the social.

The social—our context—is created and maintained by on-going conversations and behavioral patterns that are based on the stories we are taught, and we tell. Some prefer biographies, autobiographies, or a memoir. It's like watching the behavior of a person in a bottle as though the bottle didn't exist. The irony of our dominant culture is that we tell stories which create a content that ignores context. If we want to promote a climate of justice, we must listen to the stories of those who experience social injustices.

Some have taken King's saying about the content of character as an appeal to individualism. Such an interpretation, however, only makes sense in a context of white privilege. Of course, we want to be judged by the content of our character, but for most of us the content of our character depends largely on our social context.

A Conceivable Letter to People like House Representative Mike Johnson

Nov 2023

Dear Mr. Johnson,

People like me and people like you don't often talk with each other, so I thought I would write a letter to propose some topics we might talk about. I also want to share with you that from my perspective your application of Christianity prevents us from moving toward a climate of justice.

I read that you were born in Shreveport, Louisiana. I was born in Fremont, Nebraska. Different places. Have you ever wondered who you would be if you were born in India? Would you be a Hindu fundamentalist instead of a Christian fundamentalist? Can you imagine yourself as a child of a Jewish family, or a black family?

I assume you were born—born of a woman—like the rest of us. I wonder if you tried to raise your children, as we did, as fundamentally good and beautiful, or if you raised them as born in sin, as some evangelicals do. Did you try to break their will, or guide it?

You may believe that it is God's will that you were born a white child in the South. You do know that you were born in a peculiar social world, don't you? I have lived in peculiar social worlds. That's the only kind there are. We always live in some context.

You have said that we can open the Bible to know what we should do. Jesus will tell us, so to speak. Remember that Jesus was a Jew. His Jewish followers believed that he was the Messiah for whom they had been waiting. Other Jews disagreed. The point here is simple: When we are listening to Jesus, we are listening to a Jew.

We are also listening to someone who lived under Roman occupation. I think Jesus fought against the occupation, but others disagree. In any case, we are not occupied by a foreign power. We have the privilege of living, for the most part, in a democracy. Our context, in other words, is very different than the context of the Bible. (Jesus never worried about the demise of democracy.)

The denial of contextual differences may be one reason that some evangelical Christians perpetuate the tradition of the "Lost Cause' that sees the federal government as an occupier of southern states. The strong emotions behind this tradition reside in resentment, hate, and fear. The fear is the fear that propels white supremacy, and we now find it throughout our nation.

When I studied theology in graduate school, I found Paul Ricoeur's interpretative guidelines very useful for reading classical texts, like the Bible. He saw three stages: the first was a naive reading, where one believed what the text said; the second a critical stage, where one studied the text's history, its context and its purpose; and then a third stage of re-engagement with the text to discover its meaning for today. I may be wrong, but you seem to be stuck in the first stage.

People have different beliefs, but they are also persons. The danger with "true believers" is that they refuse to see any distance between their beliefs and themselves. They lose the capacity to appreciate the humanity of others because they have erased their own humanity.

In the civic sphere, there are no gods, only persons. Martin Luther King Jr. knew this, which is why he led a Civil Rights movement instead of a Christian movement. Creating a climate of justice needs religious and non-religious communities to speak for justice—to inspire the civic realm—but not to dominate it.

STEP

12

Interrupt Monocultural Thinking

The Clash of Stories on the National Mall

Feb 2020

The Museum for African American History and Culture has six floors, and most people start their visit, as I did, by taking an elevator down three floors that brings you to the beginning of the African American experience of living in America. You then walk from the ground floor to the third floor through multiple exhibits, from the Atlantic slave trade, through the horrors of slavery, the Jim Crow era, to the civil rights movements.

The top three floors about the ground floor are exhibits of African American contributions in the arts and letters, culture and sports. These exhibits erase any line that would separate contemporary American culture from the creativity of African Americans. At the same time, at least for me, these exhibits did not erase my memory of the violations of humanity exhibited on the lower three floors.

The Museum of African American History and Culture belongs on the National Mall like the Holocaust memorial belongs in the center of Berlin. They tell a truth about a nation's crimes against humanity. The African American Museum also makes us consider its place among the other monuments. We remember that Washington and Jefferson bought and sold enslaved human beings. They participated in crimes against humanity.

That's not the story most of us learned in school. We did learn that Thomas Jefferson wrote The Declaration of Independence. He also owned a slave labor farm (plantation) of around 200 enslaved people and on top of that raped a 14-year-old enslaved girl when he was 47. This clash of stories should not be ignored. Just the opposite. The clash of stories gives us a chance to work on the creation of a climate of justice

Critical White Theory

Sept 2021

Just as critical race theory tries to explain the role of race in American history, critical white theory would look at the role of white supremacy. White supremacy, in other words, is a "role," or social behavior, not a skin color. Critical white theory, from this perspective, provides answers to such questions as "Why did they do that?" by indicating the role that person assumed. "They were acting White."

One of the chief characteristics of the white social role is to behave as though other peoples and cultures did not exist. That's what it means to be monocultural in a multicultural context. The result, of course, is that others are invisible. They do not matter.

Given our beginning as a slave nation with ideals of liberty, this contradiction has a long legacy. Instead of seeing ourselves as one among others, we only saw ourselves. At the same time, this "non-social" image was and is unstable because it is not only based on a lie, but also on crimes against humanity. The white social world perpetuates a climate of injustice.

A good example of monocultural thinking in a multicultural context is the Supreme Court Justice, Amy Coney Barrett's interpretative theory of originalism, which assumes that the original meaning of the Constitution is its meaning today. This theory assumes that the

Constitution exists apart from its context, and that any contemporary reader should read the text outside of any context.

Texts, from this perspective, are not "social documents" written in a particular time and place, but rather "isolated documents" without a history, so to speak. Originalism assumes that one's particular social identity doesn't exist, and neither does the social identity of others. Critical white theory would point out that the denial of the social is a characteristic of white social identity, and regardless of any person's intention, maintains the lie that only white roles matter.

The fact is that the context of the Constitution was a climate of injustice, and that climate continues. Extracting the Constitution from this messy legacy will not help us to move toward a climate of justice.

I see a similar dilemma in President Biden's responses to our moral failures, like the incident of border patrol officers using their horses to "corral" Haitian immigrants. Biden said the images were horrific, and "That's not who we are." Critical white theory would look at this behavior from the social and historical legacy of white supremacy and probably conclude "that's exactly who we are."

The issue is not merely historical consciousness, but even more the question of who is included in Biden's "we." If the "we" are only white Americans, then such behavior can be seen as a violation of American ideals. If the "we" also include black and brown Americans, then the images may show us once again that we have not yet made the change that's been promised.

"We the People" was written in a climate of injustice. It included some white men, who made the necessary compromises to keep others out so they could enjoy American prosperity. We have always been multiracial and multicultural, but not a multiracial and multicultural democracy. Why not? Because the prosperity of the few was based on the suffering of the many.

Once again, the agenda of creating a multiracial and multicultural democracy has been put aside and whites—liberal and conservative— focus on another compromise that will ensure American prosperity, white privilege, and an American monoculture.

Whose History is Upon Us?

July 2022

Whose history is upon us? Right now, the history of white America seems to have gained control of the Supreme Court and much of public policy. This history, of course, maintains a climate of injustice that prevents us from responding in any adequate manner to our environmental crisis.

This climate of injustice has a long legacy, and it's hard to imagine changing our social climate without some knowledge of its history, especially the history of people who paid the price of American prosperity. Good intentions, in other words, is not enough. We also need to do our homework.

To that end, I decided to put together a timeline of the interactions between American settlers and American Indians to show a more detailed story of what occurred since 1776.

To develop the following timeline, I followed Howard University Law Library's framework of seven eras, and then I added the dates of key events to each of the seven eras. Some events may appear self-explanatory, but many are not. You can find brief descriptions of the events at the *Native Voices* website. Also, this timeline does not include an adequate account of the implicit meaning of these events. Still, to understand who we are, we need to know what we have done. So, here it is:

A Native American Timeline: Seven Eras of Native and Settler Americans after 1776:

1. The Treaty Era (1778-1820)

> 1778: The first U.S. treaty with an American Indian tribe is ratified
>
> 1787: Congress can regulate trade with Indian tribes

1789: The Northwest Ordinance guarantees tribal land rights

The Ordinance directs that "the utmost good faith shall always be observed towards Indians: their land and property shall never be taken from them without their consent."

1794: Battle of Fallen Timbers opens Northwest Territory to settlement

1805: Tenskwatawa and Tecumseh call for unity among tribes

1809: Treaty of Fort Wayne takes 3 million acres from Native peoples

1812: War of 1812 breaks Tecumseh's resistance

2. The Removal Era (1820-1850)

1823: Supreme Court rules American Indians do not own land. At core of Supreme Court Decision was the "discovery doctrine." Native Americans were occupiers of the land, but the Europeans who had "discovered" it owned it.

1824: U.S. establishes Office of Indian Affairs in War Department

1830: President Jackson authorizes Native People's removal from Georgia

1832: Winnebago-U.S. treaty promises a doctor (Of the 389 treaties with tribes that the U.S. Congress ratified, most promise to send a doctor to the tribes; some promise to operate hospitals for the tribes.)

1832: Supreme Court rules U.S. must treat tribes as nations

1838: Cherokee die on Trail of Tears

1849: Indian Affairs moves to Interior Department

3. The Reservation Era (1850-1887)

> 1851: Congress creates reservations to manage Native peoples
>
> 1864: The Navajos begin 'Long Walk' to imprisonment
>
> 1864: Citizen-army massacres Sand Creek women, children
>
> 1868: President Grant advances "Peace Policy" with tribes
>
> 1868: Navajo internment ends, but 2,000 died while imprisoned
>
> 1868: U.S. treaty count with American Indian tribes reaches 367
>
> 1868: Fort Laramie Treaty promises to provide health care, services
>
> 1870: First Ghost Dance movement seeks revival of cultures
>
> 1872: General Mining Act gives rise to the taking of tribal lands
>
> 1876: Custer defeated; Lakota and Cheyenne prevail
>
> 1879: First off-reservation boarding school for Native children opens
>
> 1879: Standing Bear argues for Poncas in federal court
>
> 1883: Courts of Indian Offenses established

4. The Allotment and Assimilation Era (1887-1934)

> 1887: U.S. subdivides reservation land; sells off surplus
>
> 1887: Indian Affairs Commissioner bans Native languages in schools
>
> 1889: Second Ghost Dance movement widespread among tribes
>
> 1890: U.S. Cavalry massacres Lakota at Wounded Knee
>
> 1890: Native population plunges
>
> 1898: Boarding-school epidemics sicken students and kill many

1898: U.S. annexes Hawaii; seizes land; suppresses healers

1917: More Indians are born than die

1918-19: 'Spanish Influenza' claims millions of lives

1924: American Indians granted U.S. citizenship

5. The Self-Government Era (1934-1953)

1934: Commissioner calls for religious freedom for American Indians

1934: President Franklin Roosevelt signs the Indian Reorganization Act

1941: Hawaii under martial law; U.S. military takes sacred lands

1942: Code talkers relay secret military messages during WWII

1944: National Congress of American Indians established

1946: Judicial commission adjudicates Native land claims

1947: Office of Indian Affairs upgraded to bureau

6. The Termination Era (1953-1970)

1953: Congress seeks to abolish tribes, relocate American Indians

1957: Cello Falls fishery, village destroyed by Dalles Dam

1968: American Indian Movement advocates for urban Indian rights

1968: President Johnson signs the Indian Civil Rights Act

1969: 'Indians of All Tribes' group occupies Alcatraz Island

7. The Self-Determination Era (1970-2004)

> 1970: Termination era ends: self-determination proposed
>
> 1973: American Indian Movement occupies Wounded Knee
>
> 1974: Study finds American Indian women forcibly sterilized
>
> 1974: Indian self-determination becomes the law of the land
>
> 1976: Government admits unauthorized sterilization of Indian Women
>
> 1980: Maine Indians settle land claims against U.S
>
> 1988 Indian Gaming Regulatory Act
>
> 1990: 'NAGPRA' (Native American Graves Protection and Repatriation Act) requires return of sacred remains and objects
>
> 1991: Tribal self-government expanded
>
> 1993: President Clinton apologizes for 1893 overthrow of Hawaiian monarchy
>
> 2004: The National Museum of the American Indian opens in Washington, DC.

Since 2004, of course, the multiple trends of this timeline continue to shape our future. The question is whether our historical knowledge of ourselves helps us understand what we need to change to move from a climate of injustice to a climate of justice.

Telling Multiple Stories

Oct 2022

As we approach the mid-terms, more than one commentator has framed the key question as "who controls the narrative." One might think that the key questions are about such issues as rising inflation, saving our democracy, immigration, voting rights, or government control of women's lives. Are narratives more important?

For those who know the truth, narratives may not seem important. Still, one should remember that while the truth might well set you free, what the truth means resides in its story. After all, the early Christian church needed four narratives of Jesus's life to clarify the meaning of the Gospel.

To tell the truth about the United States, four stories are probably not enough. I used to ask my students to write a one-page story of the United States. You might try it sometime. They wrote stories of early migrations from Asia, European conquest, Westward expansion, technological developments, wars and more wars, enslavement of millions, writing the Constitution, and more. I said that all the stories were true, but some were more helpful than others in creating our future.

During a visit this past summer to Vienna, Austria, we visited the Hundertwasser Museum, where I found one saying that I particularly liked:

If we do not honour our past, we lose our future.
If we destroy our roots, we cannot grow.

As you probably know, I don't think we can grow—grow up I would say—until we change our social climate to a climate of justice. Let's face it, our "roots" are entangled in and will grow out of the 400-year relationships among the undeserved misery and the unearned prosperity of "We, the People." We will not grow up until we straighten out these roots, which will entail reconciliation, reparations, and restoration.

Some don't want us to grow up. They like the idea of patriarchy. If they control the narrative, which means prohibiting others from telling their stories, we will all suffer and so will the planet.

We must be careful in discerning what storytellers assume about their listeners. Do they want their listeners to become "true believers," or appreciative inquirers? Do they create a vision that honors the limits of the Earth? Do their stories invite us to have empathy for the vulnerable? Do they, in some small way, move us toward a climate of justice?

Abolish White Supremacy

Education for White People

June 2020

To engage in the work of creating a climate of justice based on the repair of social relations and mutual recognition, we need to overcome a major obstacle: white supremacy. It would be a mistake to put all white persons in the same box, but we need to acknowledge that the box (a white privileged social world) exists. We may not be able to get out of the box, but we can become aware of it. Such awareness includes not only a critical analysis of the white social world's patterns and on-going conversations, but also critical reflection of how this social world has shaped our beliefs. Learning about this white social world as a white person is an educational process that includes the following steps:

1. Distinguish between personal and social stories
2. Explore the sources of white arrogance
3. Talk about how you have benefited from racism
4. Get in touch with your vulnerabilities
5. Listen to how others see you
6. Compose stories that include all Americans
7. Participate in the creation of a climate of justice

Because of the strong individualism of American culture, it's easy for individuals to take any criticism of white racism as a criticism of them. In fact, the libertarian strain of the white social world prevents one from seeing that libertarianism itself is a social phenomenon.

Once we grasp the difference between social and personal stories, we can begin to examine the sources of white arrogance, which Robin DiAngelo has somewhat paradoxically exposed as "white fragility." White arrogance, in other words, is not based on strength but on defending the hypocrisy of the white-only story. The white social world, after all, exists in a climate of injustice caused by the enslavement and displacement of millions during the Atlantic commerce.

If you grew up as I did, this climate of injustice did not chill your body, but it did chill the bodies of others. We can be aware of this chill, however, if we are willing to listen. Listening to others allows us to take in different experiences of living in America, which broadens our framework for interpreting our history and ourselves. Whether I participate in this work with others depends on whether I am trustworthy enough to be invited, which depends, in the final analysis, on the work I have done in understanding myself.

With this broader and deeper personal and social understanding, we can listen to and tell stories that reveal relationships that need repair, and thereby participate in changing our political culture from a climate of injustice to a climate of justice. A change that is necessary not only for our social relationships but also our relationship with the Earth.

White Men of Nebraska

Oct 2020

So, what are white men good for? They seem to be good for Trump. According to recent pieces by Michael Sokolove (10/25) and Charles M. Blow (10/26) in the New York Times, they are the group that gives Trump a chance to win, provided they are sufficiently angry and resentful to vote in large numbers.

119

I certainly do not belong to this group, but as a white man of Nebraska, I have to consider what happened to them that did not happen to me. Let's consider the "Great Seal of the State of Nebraska." A man takes up the center of the seal. Not just anyone, but a blacksmith. Strange as it may seem, among other things, my father was a blacksmith, and I learned the trade working with him during the summers when I attended college. I learned how to heat metal in a forge and to reshape it with a heavy hammer on an anvil.

Above the blacksmith you read: "Equality Before the Law." Imagine: Nine years before the Battle of the Little Big Horn (1876) and twenty-three years before the Wounded Knee Massacre in 1890, Nebraskans 'believed" in "equality before the law." This should be a clue about what happened to some white men in Nebraska.

The seal is filled with agriculture products, the Missouri River, the railroad, and the Rocky Mountains in the background.

What happened to some white men in Nebraska is that they took this picture as the truth. They didn't see what was sealed off: the Pawnee communities that lived on this territory for generations, the Sioux who fought to save it for their communities, the Chinese who built the railroad, the African Americans who provided cheap labor, the women who made human life possible, the families who created homes, and the Earth as a living system. This was the world of good men, who believed in "equality before the *white* man's law."

Now, the seal has been broken. (Excuse the play on words) The picture was a lie. It's not that white men do not belong in the picture. Others belong as well. The white man's fear, of course, is that they will no longer be at the center. Here is one of the many paradoxes: Even though the picture shows abundance, the mentality of scarcity dominates the white man's world.

In fact, the most important things in life don't decrease through sharing; they increase. White men will not have less. They will actually have more. Still, there is resistance to breaking the seal for a variety of reasons. It will be broken, and what will happen next is unknown.

The White Storm

May 2021

Some of us thought that President Biden's victory would take the wind out of the White Storm, but that became wishful thinking after the January insurrection. Now, the storm intensifies, posing a threat to our democracy.

In a way, this storm is a repetition of hurricanes and tornadoes that have been an integral part of our history since the Atlantic commerce of land and people. Recent scholarship gives more and more credence to the theory that even the American Revolution was partially propelled by the White Storm. The British government was already talking about the abolition of slavery and the Treaty of 1763 limited the expansion of the colonies beyond the border of "Indian Territory." It certainly took over after the Reconstruction period in the mythology of the "Lost Cause." We may not be able to calm it. But we can protect our democracy from it.

Just like Red Flag warnings will not eliminate California fires, they make us aware of the danger and in some cases, may save homes and lives. In the same way, "Red Flags" will not eliminate the White Storm, but they will keep us aware and awake. Wouldn't it be nice if we could all work together? Wouldn't it be nice if we still had two political parties whose disagreements could be addressed through rational debate? The trumpet has been sounded. It's time to take cover and to protect the vulnerable. Let's face it, you don't fight a storm; you protect yourself from it.

How do we do this? First, we protect the vulnerable. That means today that we make sure everyone has full access to our democracy, which means passing the "For the People Act." We must also protect civilians from police brutality and abuse and provide care for those in need; that means passing the George Floyd Justice in Policing Act. Secondly, we must enforce the rule of law. When possible, we must hold people, like Trump, accountable for their crimes. Criminal justice may be slow, but it must be steady and trustworthy.

I know, some believe that we can take the wind out of the White Storm by giving people jobs or money. The White Storm is not an economic problem. It's not an individual problem. It's a social problem that does not have a social solution. The solution requires a civic engagement in the formulation of public policies that are grounded in the "promise" of our democracy.

The Abolition of the Master Class

June 2021

Juneteenth is now a national holiday: a day to celebrate the freeing of enslaved African Americans. What has not been announced is what this means for their "masters." It stands to reason that the abolition of slavery was also the abolition of the master class. Now, that's something we could celebrate all year!

When my grandfather came to the United States, he came by way of Canada, crossed the border illegally, and eventually bought lots of Nebraska land in the 1930s. He arrived, in other words, years after the abolition of slavery, but not the abolition of the master class.

He was able to buy land, acquire loans from banks, hired "farmhands" to help with the wheat harvest. He didn't need to own enslaved people to be part of the master class. He was white. And he knew a thing or two about dealing with banks and government officials. As far as I know, he assumed that the world of the master class was as natural as raising a family or burying the dead. It was not, for him, a world that belonged to the enslavement of millions.

Masters and slaves are two sides of the same coin. The fact is that the abolition of the master class was not carried out in 1865, but rather intermeshed with American exceptionalism and the American Dream. That leaves us with work to do that should have been done years ago. Maybe Juneteenth will give us another opportunity to become a people with different social identities and a shared humanity.

Dealing with White Distortion

Dec 2021

As a white male person, I continue to deal with the issue of white distortion. Distortion is not that uncommon. Sometimes it's comical, like when we walk through a hall of mirrors. Sometimes, it's not, like when it prevents us from working together to secure our habitat.

If you grew up something like I did, then doing what seems natural can get you into a lot of trouble, or at least keep others in their troubles. White distortion is not the same for everyone. For those in the "White Power Movement" the distortion not only warps their vision, but also freezes it in place. This kind of distortion is a cult leader's dream. It's like one's mind has turned into stone.

For most of us, our white distortion is not so massive. If we work at it, we can control it instead of it controlling us. The key to understanding everyday white distortion is to recognize that one does not see it from the inside. White distortion doesn't appear distorted to white people. The power that arises from being white in a white man's world, in other words, seems "natural." From the white perspective, differences don't really matter because we are all individuals.

In his book, *Inventing the Individual*, Larry Siedentop attributes individualism to the West's replacement of family and local gods with Christian monotheism (2015). Just like there was one God, every person was one person with one soul. This soul was deeper than any family and social identity. Siedentop's historical analysis ends with the beginning of the modern age when secular thinkers borrowed this religious individualism to develop what we know as modern liberalism.

Siedentop's story seems true enough until one notices the absence of any sociological analysis. He writes as though the social did not exist. His logic is fine: God created all of us, so we are all equal. That's the kind of thinking one gets when you practice theology without sociology. Sociology does not deny a shared humanity, but it looks at our humanity as embedded in social relations.

If one interprets Christianity from the perspective of the white distortion, it looks a lot like capitalism in that it extracts persons from social relations and sees them as isolated entities. The white distortion omits from its framework our social relations, which serve as the matrix and source of individual development. When these social relations exist in a legacy of racial oppression and violence, as they do today, the white distortion also covers up white racism.

Ignoring these relations does have its consequences. It means that white people in Europe and America have a distorted view of themselves and the world in which they live. Many of us now see how the West has constructed a world that erases our relationships with each other and with the Earth. It's not that difficult to recognize the long history of the cult of white supremacy that has been recently stoked by Trump and his cohorts. I think we are slowly learning how to deal with this through the enforcement of the rule of law and the protection of voting rights. These struggles are now entering a decisive phase.

The larger issue is the continuing process of correcting the distorted vision of our national identity. Roxanna Dunbar-Ortiz's new book, *NOT A Nation of Immigrants: Settler Colonialism, White Supremacy, and A History of Erasure and Exclusion,* shines a light on many aspects of our history that our white view has omitted. I think her point is that it's a distortion of the truth to name European conquerors and enslavers "immigrants" to the Americas.

Dealing with such distortions would be a good step in preparing ourselves for cooperating with others in creating a climate of justice.

Writing While White

Jan 2022

It's true that my book *A Climate of Justice* was written by a white man. Is that significant? Some white people, of course, might not see their work as written by a white person, because they don't see whiteness. They just see individuals or humans, but they never see the social worlds in which they exist.

To see myself as a white writer, I must have created some distance between my person and my white social world. I don't think I recognized this gap in any meaningful way until I was in college. Such social amnesia is a white person's privilege that is maintained by paying attention to some stories and ignoring others.

Even with this critical distance between myself and my social world, I am still a "white writer." So, what does that mean? Well, it means I am not a Black writer or a Native American writer. My writing is not embedded in their social worlds, but in a white social world. And what kind of social world is that?

In *A Climate of Justice*, I define it as a social world that privileges whites over others, denies that others suffered and continue to suffer for these privileges, and justifies this condition by asserting white superiority. All this results in what I call a "climate of injustice."

White writers, as I see it, could know that they write in this social world. How do they do that? Let me use Aristotle's four causes to answer that question. Aristotle's four causes are material, efficient, formal, and final. The usual illustration is a statue. The material cause is the stone, the efficient cause is the sculptor, the formal cause is the implicit or possible shape in the stone, and the final cause is the purpose of the work. The causes are answers to the question, "Why does something exist?" The answer is "be-cause" of the material used, the worker's work, the inherent design in the materials, and the purpose.

In the Acknowledgments in *A Climate of Justice*, I write about my "mindfulness." The knowledge from many others filled my mind with different perspectives and critical stances. This would be the material cause. I am grateful for receiving this knowledge and I also recognize that my access to this knowledge is a privilege for those of us who existed in or could enter a white social world.

The efficient cause focuses on me as a writer. Writing a book like *A Climate of Justice* involves not only the writer's character, but also the writer's implicit readers and the development of arguments. Aristotle refers to these three elements as ethos, pathos, and logos—the identity of the writer, the values of the audience, and the logic of the speech.

Writing, in other words is a relational activity that expresses what is thought-provoking in the interplay of self, other, and language.

So, who are the others, or what literary critics call a writer's "implied audience"? For the most part, I write to other white people—people who exist in our unjust white social world. I advance the possibility that my readers could be invited to meet those who have carried the burden of white privilege in a civic sphere where broken relationships could be repaired.

In this transformation from social worlds to civic spheres, I have given myself as well as my readers a space to relate to me not as white but rather as a member of the civic. For the most part, I am a citizen with the responsibility to support the rule of law that protects and provides for civilians who are vulnerable and cannot protect themselves. This does not erase my white social world, but rather gives me a place to join with others in dealing with it.

"Writing while white" has a couple of meanings. It acknowledges my belonging to the social world constructed by the legacy of white supremacy. At the same time, this social identity exists "only for a while," because it is possible that I can move into a civic sphere when invited by civilians, to write as a citizen. To realize this possibility for myself and my readers is the "final cause" or purpose of *A Climate of Justice*.

The White Dream of Safety

July 2022

Like everyone else, white people dream of safety. The desire for safety, in fact, may be as strong if not stronger than other primal drives. When we consider whiteness as a social category the problem arises that the white dream of safety depends on the continued maintenance of a climate of injustice.

One could see the white dream of safety as part and parcel of the American Dream. If you think about it, most immigrants or settlers were not drawn to the US by a dream of justice, but rather by a dream of safety—a dream that splits off from consciousness the misery that has been caused by that dream.

Like others, Trump followers can also be seen as caught in a white dream of safety. For them, the findings of the January 6 committee not only threaten their beliefs but also their safety. When safety is based on a lie, truth is the enemy.

I know that people say, "The truth will set you free," but who wants to be free from safety? Better in a boat of true believers than in the water alone.

Freedom does not offer safety, but justice does. Justice comes in twos and threes and in communities. It never comes alone. When those who are unsafe, who are vulnerable, seek to tell us the truth—to expose the lies of white supremacy—they offer us the safety of justice.

If we lived in a climate of justice, the white dream of safety would be seen as a relic of our past that has been discarded for the safety of justice. We are not there yet, and the results of the midterms will tell us if we are moving in that direction.

Distribute Provisions Fairly

What part of corporations do you want to stimulate?

Mar 2020

The most controversial aspect of the congressional stimulus package evolves around its "help" to corporations. As I understand it, the legislation permits the Federal Reserve to offer cheap loans to corporations of almost unlimited amounts. So, what aspects of corporations is this package supposed to stimulate?

In my book *Corporate Integrity,* I first defined corporations as social entities, which is to say that they are creations of ongoing communication patterns and behaviors, and you can change them by changing these patterns. This means they are not biological entities or biological persons. (The Supreme Court made all of this very confusing by evidently not understanding the distinction between biological and legal "persons.") That's another story. In any case, a clear description of a corporation needs to include five dimensions: the legal, property, communal, social, and environmental.

Corporations are legal creations. Most American corporations have charters from Delaware, which gives them the right to engage in assigned activities. These laws can be changed, and probably should be. We really need a national charter for corporations. The point is that corporations are always subject to civic control.

The laws allow us to treat corporations as property. They can be bought and sold. "Public" corporations allow investors to purchase stock, which initially gives the previous owners capital and later gives managers leverage to borrow money. For stockholders, the value of a corporation depends on the fate of its stock price. That's not true for other corporate stakeholders.

Corporations are not just property. They are also places of work. These places provide a location for the development of community, meaning, and well-being, depending on the design of the workplace. In contrast to the corporation as a legal entity, the corporate workplace is grounded in biological personhood. Even though corporations are property, it is a moral mistake to treat workers in the same way.

Corporations are also social entities, and they have a social function or purpose. If you ask why automobile companies exist, the answer is found by looking at the transformation system and defining their purpose within it. As I argued in *Civilizing the Economy*, the primary purpose of corporations is determined by their role in a civic economy designed to provide people with what they need. Corporations, in other words, are providers.

Finally, corporations belong to and are part and parcel of the natural environment. They extract from the planet and return waste to it. They increase or decrease global warming. They influence the future habitat for our children and grandchildren.

So given these different dimensions, what should our government stimulate?

Farm Loyalty and Meat Processing Plants

May 2020

When I was a kid on our family farm in Nebraska, my brother and I made sure that my calf would grow up to become a well-fed cow. Raising the calf was one of my 4-H projects, and he received a blue ribbon at the county fair. I didn't remember the 4-H pledge (the four Hs of head, heart, hands, and health), so I looked it up:

I pledge my head to clearer thinking
My heart to greater loyalty
My hands to larger service
And my health to better living
for my club, my community, my country and my world.

I have tried to keep the first pledge, but the second not so well. Loyalty, of course, has a lot of meanings, but if we remember that it comes in the pledge after "clearer thinking," then its more positive meaning may become available. In light of the current reign of the coronavirus in the meat processing plants throughout our country, I wonder if I and many others have been disloyal to farming and farming communities.

Sometimes the idea of loyalty sounds like the opposite of "clearer thinking." That's blind loyalty. Thoughtful loyalty means remaining connected; not abandoning and dismissing. Like many others, I left the farm, which seems OK, but I think I also abandoned farming—at least until I began working on my book *Civilizing the Economy.*

There I proposed that we examine different systems of provision, such as the food system, and design the system not only to make provisions for all, but also to protect human and non-human providers. From a systems perspective, it's clear that the connection between raising calves and eating them needs to be recognized as promoting either a climate of justice or injustice.

When we sold my calf, I petted him and said good-by. I remember feeling sad, but not like I or my calf had been violated. Nor was I troubled by eating the chickens I killed, and my mother cooked, or the corn I picked from the sweet corn stocks. If I had been asked, I would have said that these plants and animals were alive, and it was OK to eat them. In a way, the 4-H pledge, as well as the teaching of my parents, provided the context for living on the farm.

Family farms in Nebraska, of course, belonged to a different world than that of the brutal slaughterhouses that Upton Sinclair described in his 1906 novel *The Jungle*, which exposed the owner's shocking treatment of both animals and workers. While there are local farms today that have some resemblance to our family farm, the world of Concentrated Animal Feeding Operations (CAGOs) and JBS's meat processing plants have stark similarities with the slaughterhouses that Sinclair exposed more than a century ago.

Over a third of the workers at the Nebraska meat processing plants are undocumented workers. Trump has called their work "essential," and ordered the plants to remain open. These are workers without health care, without any civic rights, and dependent on wages. And, of course, they do not have the right to vote. Even the information they need is only given in English and sign language, while they speak Spanish! Still, the workers return to work knowing they could catch COVID 19. Talk about a climate of injustice!!!

The plants themselves belong to global businesses. Some of the plants in Nebraska belong to JBS, a Brazilian company that is the largest meat producer in the world.

JBS was founded a little over 60 years ago by Jose Batista Sobrinho (therefore: JBS) and is now run by his two sons. Much of its expansion in the United States was financed with low-interest bank loans. The brothers later admitted in a plea deal that they had bribed bank and government officials to obtain them. With these loans, they purchased their first US meat plants in 2007, and now, with three other meat processing corporations, they control 80 percent of the meat processing in the United States. Since 2007, JBS has spent more than $7.7 million on lobbying and has won more than $900 million in government meat contracts, according to the Washington Post.

US meat packing plants belong to a global animal and animal parts trading network. It turns out that almost half of "grass-fed" beef in the United States is imported from Australia, most of it by JBS. One could assume that if it is "grass-fed, then the cows would be raised locally. The label "product of USA," however, does not say where the cows are raised, but where they were processed.

Do we want to know this? As many of us are turning to "impossible beef" or other plant-based foods, the beef is not on our plate, so to speak. Farm loyalty, however, does not mean eating meat. It does mean not denying our systemic relationship with each other, other animals, and the Earth. JBS belongs to a world that is not only using its scale of operations to put small and local farmers out of business, managing meat processing plants dependent on disenfranchised workers, but also advancing the destruction of the Brazilian rain forests to raise more cattle.

A group of farmers have formed the "Agriculture Fairness Alliance" and petitioned Congress to dismantle the meat processing oligarchy and to protect small farmers. Their work would seem to move us toward a climate of justice.

Elizabeth Warren and others have pledged to break up the largest food and meat companies because they use their "economic power to spend unlimited sums of money electing and manipulating politicians" and because they are "leaving family farmers with fewer choices, thinner margins and less independence." Not much like the 4-H pledge, but maybe a good expression of farm loyalty.

Who Will Pay for This?

June 2020

Good question. But not answerable until we know who or what is included in the "this." In fact, you could probably do a bias check by noting what initially came to mind when you read the question.

The "this" could be:

- Hospitals' costs of caring for COVID-19 patients
- 50 States' costs of providing services for the epidemic
- Businesses' cost of repair from looting
- Cost of providing basic food security
- Cost of unemployment
- Cost of losses in the stock market

- Cost of losses in public education
- Cost of shifting from a military to a civilian approach to social problems

How do you decide? We may not be having a revolution, but we are in the midst of a revelation—a revelation of a lot that needs repair and reform. The pandemic has revealed the inequality in health care, the lack of protection for essential workers, and the heroes who have risked their lives for the rest of us. And then civilian responses to the murder of Floyd George revealed that current patterns of civilian-police relations must be transformed.

So how do we decide what the "this" is? We have to decide what matters, or what matters in such a way that caring for it will bring other matters in its wake. Black lives matter; or to put it in another form, if black lives don't matter, nothing matters.

So, once we know which costs matter, we can then figure out how to get the money to pay for them. For the most part, we can either take it or create it. We could take money from financial speculators, property owners, and national budgets.

- Speculators and investors who got rich from other people's work and assets.
- Property owners who have "unearned income" from the increase of property value due to the dynamics of social systems and public policy.
- National budgets that could direct funds toward civilian security instead of national security.

As a rule, it is better to create money than to take it, especially when you need it immediately. That's what governments can do. On March 25th, Congress passed a 2 trillion-dollar stimulus package in response to the coronavirus epidemic. The House passed a $3 trillion-dollar package in April. That money was not taken. It was created.

So, how is this money created? The government sells government bonds to the large banks that belong to the Federal Reserve. The banks create the money to buy the bonds, which they then exchange for them, and then the government promises to repay with interest, which becomes a government debt. The government, in other words, facilitates the creation of money by borrowing it from the banks. The banks profit from the transaction by getting interest on the debt.

As you might wonder, why doesn't the government create its own money, which would eliminate not only interest payments but government debt? The Public Banking Institute has some proposals for moving in that direction that are worth considering. For now, it's safe to say that if the government can create millions or trillions for preventing economic collapse, it can also create money to cover the costs for things that matter.

Prosperity and Justice

Aug 2021

Is justice necessary for prosperity or can we aim for prosperity now and leave justice for later? Can the good crowd out the right? If some of us have jobs and childcare, will we ignore that others have lost the right to vote?

From the Atlantic commerce of people and land to the current climate crisis, the West has lived as though prosperity could thrive without justice. It turns out, however, that's not the only tradition that could control our future.

Linda Darling's book *A History of Social Justice and Political Power in the Middle East: The Circles of Justice from Mesopotamia to Globalization* (Routledge, 2013) gives us a different perspective to think about the future. She traces the long history of the Middle Eastern notion of the "circles of justice" that put justice before prosperity.

The notion of a circle of justice goes back to the earliest Mesopotamian kingdoms, beginning with Sumer and Akkad and ending with the Islamic revolution. In some form, it existed for over 4 millennia. The Circle of Justice did have various formulations, but also a few consistent principles, such as "the strong might not oppress the weak". This principle did not exist as an isolated commandment, of course, but rather as part of Middle Eastern wisdom of how to govern. One early formulation quoted in many Middle Eastern works had these four sentences:

No power without troops,
No troops without money,
No money without prosperity
No prosperity without justice and good administration.

Justice, in other words, is the basis for prosperity; prosperity allows people to pay taxes that can provide money to pay the troops, and the troops ensure power (of the sovereign).

Justice is the basis for prosperity because the workers (peasants) will only be productive when treated fairly. As Darling writes: "The Near Eastern concept of state saw the ruler as far above the elites, the ally of the peasants against both elites and outside forces." This meant not only that the state would build waterways and infrastructure so the farmers could be productive, but also that they would hear petitions from the peasants when they had complaints.

This was not exactly a Civilian Review Board, but one can imagine something like it to make a comparison with our civilian institutions.

There are other formulations of the circles of justice. Darling quotes a common rendition from the 10th century:

The world is a garden, hedged in by sovereignty
Sovereignty is lordship, preserved by law
Law is administration, governed by the king
The King is a shepherd, supported by the army
The army are soldiers, fed by money
Money is revenue, gathered by the people
The people are servants, subjected by justice
Justice is happiness, the well-being of the world.

As we know, the modern West, whose fate was sealed by the Atlantic commerce of people, land, and products, chose prosperity over justice. In fact, its prosperity was founded on injustice. This caused what I call a climate of injustice that has never been fully repaired.

At the same time, our democratic beliefs and practices certainly offer a different option than that of the rulers of the Middle Eastern kingdoms. Despite the potential for our democratic institutions to advance justice, they have consistently prioritized prosperity over justice. Now that prosperity is destroying the planet, we not only see our moral failure but also the need for a different approach.

Western imperialism and its aftermath have made all of this very complicated. Still, we need all the help we can get, and maybe the wisdom of the "circles of justice" can at least open us to the possibility that prosperity without justice will fail to save the planet.

How To Protect What We Share

Oct 2020

First lesson from 2020: We cannot protect what we have without protecting what we share. In Southern Oregon, fires destroyed the small towns of Phoenix and Talent. Both homeowners in new condominiums and immigrant farmworkers in trailer parks lost what that had. They could not protect what they had because they could not protect what they shared. They could not protect their town.

The pandemic provides us with similar lessons. Over 210,000 have lost their lives. Many of these deaths were unnecessary. They occurred because we failed to protect what we share: the air we breathe. It's not a lack of knowledge here, but a lack of care. During the initial months, Covid-19 rapidly spread throughout the air, prompting us to adopt masks, not for personal protection but to safeguard the shared air. Authorities also failed to share medical knowledge and equipment. This failure, however, reveals a deeper one: a failure to protect those who risked their lives to care for others.

We have not only failed to protect our communities and the air; we have also failed to protect our public discourse. Lies and distortions, the denial of scientific knowledge, and boasting and roasting have all diminished the possibility of giving each other the benefit of the doubt and of trusting each other. Public discourse relies on a shared assumption that words have meanings, sentences make sense, and it is worthwhile to listen. It's probably true that Hilary Clinton's inability to safeguard public discourse prevented her from becoming our president. Let's hope we are smarter this time.

There are really two dimensions of sharing: the sharing of things and relationships of sharing. Before the fires destroyed the towns in Oregon, I would guess that the homeowners and immigrant farmworkers were not aware that they shared their town. Or that they shared the Earth. Could the experience of sharing the town's destruction cause them to explore and develop a sharing relationship?

A sharing relationship does not require that everyone gets the same. That's not true of parents and children, of artists and audiences, or of teachers and students. Instead, it means that relationships are balanced. They are based on reciprocity. Participants find that sharing benefits everyone.

In a climate of justice, sharing would seem quite reasonable. It would be a relationship based on cooperation, not competition, and on mutual respect, not superior/inferior. It would be the opposite of the divisiveness that Trump's White House spreads like a deadly disease.

So, what should we do? We could construct shelters, but this would only safeguard us, not the air, earth, cities, or public discourse. To protect these things, we need to target what is making them harmful to us and then to eliminate the causes. We will probably not take on these projects, however, until we begin to move from relationships based on competition and exclusion to relationships based on cooperation and sharing. If we see what we share, then why not see each other?

How Should We Share the Crop?

Nov 2021

Sharecropping has a bad reputation not because it's a bad idea, but because it was not protected from exploitation. In fact, it's a good idea, but it only works in a climate of justice.

After Black soldiers won the Civil War, they wanted "forty acres and a mule," which they deserved but didn't get. They didn't want to work for wages because it looked too much like a return to slavery. The third option was sharecropping. As the historian Eric Foner has pointed out, sharecropping seemed to fit the bill.

> While sharecropping did not fulfill blacks desire for full economic autonomy, the end of planters' coercive authority over the day-to-day lives of their tenants represented a fundamental shift in the balance of power in rural society, and afforded blacks a degree of control over their time, labor, and family arrangements inconceivable under slavery.
>
> *Reconstruction: American's Unfinished Revolution 1863 – 1877.* New York: Perennial Classics, 2002, p. 406

The basic idea was that farmers would contribute their labor, and the landowner would contribute the land and the seed. When the farmers didn't have their own tools, the landowner provided them and sometimes a mule to grow and harvest the crop. The crop was then shared, usually 50/50.

Although this looked like a good deal, it didn't turn out that way. Until the harvest, the sharecroppers relied on the landowner's credit, which led to the confiscation of their share of the crop to settle their debts. They were also forced to buy provisions from a company store and to sell their share to the company owners. Consequently, the dominance of white landowners smothered the black farmers desire for a place and a space.

I propose that the past gives us places from which we could imagine a different future than the one we are facing, and the sharecropper's desire and vision is such a place. Their vision of living with the Earth and with each other could give us possibilities today. No better formulation of this vision than the Creed of the Southern Tenant Farmers Union:

> All actual tillers of the soil should be guaranteed possession of the land, either as working farm families or cooperative associations of such farm families:
>
> The Earth is the common heritage of all, and the use and occupancy of the land should constitute the sole title thereto; This organization is dedicated to the complete abolition of tenantry and wage slavery in all its forms, and to the establishment of a new order of society wherein all who are willing to work shall be given the full products of their toil.
>
> in "Introduction: The Southern Tenant Farmers' Union: A Movement for Social Emancipation," in Kester, H. *Revolt Among The Sharecroppers.* Knoxville: The University of Tennessee Press, 1997

One lesson we learned from the pandemic is that we are all dependent on workers. Remember the "essential workers"? These workers include bus drivers, clerks, caregivers in nursing homes, and garbage collectors. They kept the city alive. They were "essential." In a climate of justice, they would receive their due.

Sharecropping in the United States is not the only story of sharecropping. It has been practiced throughout the world. In the nineteenth century, the philosopher John Stuart Mill wrote about the success of sharecropping in Northern Italy, citing its foundation in cooperation rather than competition. In this case, both farm workers and farm owners belonged to the same community.

Sharecropping does rest on the assumption that relationships among unequals can be fair. Not everyone is the same. There are laborers and owners, renters and landlords, even doctors and patients. There are social differences. In a climate of justice, these groups would cooperate with each other for the benefit of all.

If we were so lucky! In our climate of injustice, the more powerful exploit the more vulnerable. That's the history of sharecropping in the United States. And it's not just cotton. It's also housing and company profit. It's all forms of exchange between people and groups who are socially unequal. The question: "How should we share the crop?" has never been more relevant than it is today.

Given our current climate of injustice, we should not expect white supremacists and their ilk to cooperate with today's "sharecroppers." They haven't done so in the past, and it's likely they won't in the future. Cooperation, of course, would be nice. In its absence, we must rely on the rule of law. That's what a government is for: to promote justice, and in this case, to protect those who are vulnerable and rely on the policies of others.

It is not a bad idea to have a share of the earth for one's family and a share of the crop for their daily needs. One way to realize it (maybe the only way) is to return to the sharecroppers' desire and vision, and this time to enforce the laws that protect their civil rights.

Let money and knowledge flow freely

Oct 2022

In a climate of justice, money and knowledge would flow freely. Instead of banks only giving money to those with an acceptable credit rating, people could get enough money to "buy" the goods and services they need for a sustainable living. Same with knowledge.

My book *A Climate of Justice* exemplifies the free flow of knowledge. Because of funding from LYRASIS, it is available as an open access book, licensed under the terms of the Creative Commons Attribution 4.0 International License. This means that anyone can not only read it, but also use the material in their research. They are just asked to tell where they got the material.

Let's face it, one cannot do much with knowledge without money, and one can do a lot of harm with money without knowledge. Additionally, while some individuals understand the necessary steps to provide housing for the homeless, they lack the financial resources to implement these actions. Some have money to influence others, but not much of an idea of what values need promotion.

The problem, of course, is that both knowledge and money are treated as commodities. "I will tell you the latest management theory for $2000.00 a day." "You can increase your pile of money by investing in farmland." The hoarding of knowledge and money maintains the gap between the "haves and have-nots," and as this gap grows, so does the resentment of the have-nots against the haves.

Modern technology has changed the sharing of knowledge. If you want to know how to fix a dishwasher, there is a video that tells you how to do it. You could always go to the public library to get a book, but now you can get it online for free if it is open access.

There is a downside to the free flow of knowledge. If writers cannot make a living from their work, only those who already have money will be able to share their creations. Look at what's happened to the music industry. Composers are no longer compensated for their creations. So, what are we to do? I think it's probably true that if we are going to share knowledge, we also need to share money.

Keynesian economic theory would not have a problem with sharing money. If people have money in their pockets or a credit line on their credit cards, they can engage in the trading of such things as food, clothing, and shelter. Money would function as a means of exchange and allow us to acquire some of our provisions through the market. Other provisions, like knowledge, would be as accessible as *A Climate of Justice*.

Public Bias

Apr 2023

Last week Twitter changed the label on NPR's (National Public Radio) Twitter account to "Government-funded Media." NPR responded by stopping its activity on Twitter because "the platform is taking actions that undermine our creditability by falsely implying that we are not editorially independent" (NYT 4/13). Do you find it a little weird that government funding undermines one's credibility? Why not the opposite? Why doesn't government funding ensure independent or at least responsible journalism?

True, government-funded projects have sometimes caused great harm. Just think of the cultural genocide of government schools on American Indian reservations. At the same time, there are many "government-funded" projects that do a lot of good.

Maybe it's a matter of terminology. Saying something is "government-funded" sounds different than to say it's "publicly funded," and yet isn't the public funded by the government?

Many of us went to public schools, but how many of us went to government schools? What if we called public facilities government facilities? Are public museums also government museums? Is the public health department really a government health department? Do we bury our dead in city cemeteries or government cemeteries?

The distrust of government, like much else in America, has its roots in the history of slavery, the Lost Cause, and the current Republican Party. From our national beginning the slave states felt threatened by a national government and agreed to the union only on condition that they held a majority in the House of Representatives. After the Civil War the ideology of the Lost Cause perpetuated distrust of national government, and that continues in much of the Republican Party today.

I doubt if a government-funded media should be without some bias. There are biases toward inclusion or exclusion, toward repairing harm or denial, toward truth-telling or lying, toward regard for others or disregard, and toward a climate of justice. If Martin Luther King Jr.

is right that the arch of the moral universe bends toward justice, then that is one bias we should support.

Frankly, I would hope that government-funded media would have a bias. It's too bad that Twitter doesn't recognize theirs.

Change Course

Resetting our American Thermostat

July 2021

Did you ever wonder what prevents us from moving closer to a climate of justice—a social predisposition for fairness? Could it be a kind of thermostat that shuts down progress when it gets uncomfortable for white people?

If there is such a thermostat, it has a long history, beginning with the writing of the Constitution in such a way that the slave states would not have to worry about the Northern states abolishing slavery. It then continued with the compromises of 1820 and 1850. The Civil War knocked out the thermostat, but it was reset after Reconstruction, in spite of the 14th and 15th Amendments.

Black communities could make some progress, but not too much, as evidenced by the massacre of Greenwood in 1921. The 1960s, of course, made whites quite uncomfortable, and it took some time for Reagan and his accomplices to reset the American thermostat to an acceptable level of injustice.

One could say that each episode of the advancement of social justice required a resetting of the thermostat. Women could vote, workers could form unions, and gays and lesbians would be respected. At the same time, a lot of Whites were getting more and more uncomfortable. For them, the American thermostat seemed out of kilter.

Then a black family occupied the White House. After that, a woman wanted to be president. The climate of injustice seemed to be disappearing, and each change increased white discomfort. Trump tried to make the American thermostat white again.

Capitalism, after all, requires a climate of injustice. Life isn't supposed to be fair. Don't play the "race card." Comfort comes with success, not justice.

So, who will reset the American thermostat? After a long history of making sure whites are comfortable by setting the thermostat low enough to maintain a climate of injustice, can we reset the thermostat to enjoy a climate of justice for all of us to be comfortable in our shared habitat?

The Pandemic and Climate Change

Mar 2020

Can we take the economic slowdown caused by the coronavirus pandemic as an occasion to design a more sustainable future? That's the question Meehan Crist addresses in her NYT's article "What the Pandemic Means for Climate Change." As you might imagine, it depends.

On the one hand, as she points out, the decrease in travel, consumption, and industrial output has decreased carbon emissions. On the other hand, restrictions have slowed down the development of renewable technologies and perhaps global conferences where nations could have moved beyond the Paris agreements. Which hand gets the upper hand, so to speak, depends on what we learn from this break in the global movement toward destroying our habitat.

Since the virus caused the break, one could repair it by defeating the epidemic and stimulating the economy. To improve something that is going in the wrong direction, however, is not very smart. We need to change direction. This break offers us a chance.

This opportunity to change direction requires that we appreciate and stay connected to the health care workers who have come forward to care for and protect us. They may not be heroes, but they are stewards and servants who care for others—not for the sake of American prosperity or the American Dream—but for the sake of the vulnerable. We all are witness to a system of care that has the potential to extend to the planet and our habitat.

This break in the momentum of economic prosperity presents us with an opportunity, not to fix the break, but to break away from the tragedy of American prosperity and move toward a viable future.

Better or Different

Jan 2021

If something is going in the wrong direction, the worst thing you can do is to "make it better."

Ok, "Build Back Better" is better than "MAGA," but I think it misses the point. What's the point? That's the question.

How can we tell when we are moving in the right direction? The "we" here is the American Empire. "Empire" may not be the right word, but it's certainly closer to the truth than using the word "nation." In a sense, when the 13 colonies (nations) joined together we could have said they formed an American Empire, something like the British Empire, only at the beginning of its domination of land and people. Now that we have military bases in 150 countries, control of territories from Guam to Puerto Rico, and are largely dominated by investors rather than citizens, naming us a "nation" is as nostalgic as naming a financial giant "Wells Fargo."

The image of the Titanic does seem appropriate. We can change the chairs, maybe even improve the conditions in the boiler rooms, but it's still heading toward destruction. The fact is that we should not try to get back on course; we need to change course. Not all at once. The ship will sink. No, we need to change carefully and with resolve from a climate of injustice to a climate of justice—a climate created by care and empathy, and also by a rigorous dismantling of white supremacy and arrogance. Empathy is not enough. It may be necessary and make us feel better, but it will not make us feel different.

Perhaps the tragedy of the COVID pandemic can help us here. White men, like me, were and are not immune from the virus. We are all vulnerable. Trump's arrogance toward the virus showcased the problem. All the families who have lost loved ones could show us the solution. The point here is to follow the lead of the vulnerable and those caring for them.

What's the point? The point is that we could be different if we let civilians give us a hand in turning the ship toward a safe harbor.

Will the Epidemic Change Social Habits?

Apr 2020

The coronavirus epidemic has certainly stopped us from doing what we usually do. Without a doubt, it has disrupted many habits and even initiated different behaviors. Waving instead of hugging. Keeping a good supply of toilet paper instead of waiting until it's needed. Talking about the bravery of health workers instead of the skills of professional athletes. The question is whether we are learning new behaviors, or just pausing and waiting for things to kick into gear again.

If the pandemic had ended by Easter, it could mean that all the deaths and sacrifices were in vain. We could have more easily buried what we learned about relationships and leadership and returned to consumption and games. Our attention to the vulnerable could turn toward the invincible. Or, as the pandemic continues into April, May, and June—and maybe longer—we may see the nurse as a role model. We may imagine social systems not for masters but for servants.

It could be that the government's package of 2 trillion dollars gives us permission to imagine what money could do if it were a public good instead of a private asset. One could imagine that caring for the planet would create jobs and community.

The disruption of old social habits is an unintended consequence of responding to the dying and protecting the living. All the sacrifice and suffering should make a difference. We could learn to turn away from the trends that are destroying our habitats and learn to live in a more modest manner with each other and the Earth. We could develop habits that fit with our shared habitat. The world's children are watching.

They Knew. So What?

Oct 2021

One might think that it's the oil, gas and coal companies that are to blame for creating our climate crisis, but as Gus Speth's book *They Knew* demonstrates, our government agencies were the ones that allowed it to happen. They not only ignored reliable scientific research, but they also supported our use and dependence on sources of energy that increased global warming.

It may be true that we get the government we deserve, but our children and grandchildren deserve something better. In demonstrations, hearings and lawsuits, young people have demanded that governments stop the destruction of the planet and protect their shared habitat. Part of the significance of Speth's book is the review of the legal case of *Julianna v United States*.

The federal government's policies of ignoring clear evidence of global warming and advancing the use of fossil fuels adversely affected the lives of 21 young plaintiffs, prompting the non-profit law firm Our Children's Trust to file a complaint in 2015. The plaintiffs belonged to the youth movement that has drawn our attention to what current environmental policies are doing to their future. To the surprise of many, in 2016, a district judge in Oregon laid out an argument that supported their case. In *Juliana v United States*, Judge Ann Aiken wrote the following:

> "This action is of a different order than the typical environmental case. It alleges that [the federal government's] actions and inactions—whether or

not they violate any specific statutory duty—have so profoundly damaged our home planet that they threaten plaintiffs' fundamental constitutional right to life and liberty.

Plaintiffs have alleged that defendants played a significant role in creating the current climate crisis, that defendants acted with full knowledge of the consequences of their actions, and that defendants have failed to correct or mitigate the harms they helped create in deliberate indifference to the injuries caused by climate change. They may therefore proceed with their substantive due process challenge to defendant's failure to adequately regulate CO_2 emissions."

I have no doubt that the right to a climate system capable of sustaining human life is fundamental to a free and ordered society.

Where a complaint alleges government action is affirmatively and substantially damaging the climate system in a way that will cause human deaths, shorten human lifespans, result in widespread damage to property, threaten human food sources, and dramatically alter the planet's ecosystem, it states a claim for a due process violation. To hold otherwise would be to say that the Constitution affords no protection against a government's knowing decision to poison the air its citizens breathe or the water its citizens drink." (Speth, 158-159).

We now know that "they knew," but so what? So, our government has violated the rights of its people, and if judges uphold the rule of law, there will be consequences. Since 2016, the case has encountered one barrier after another, but it is still on its feet. If you would like to keep track of future developments visit Our Children's Trust's website.

While the future of this case is unknown, it has increased our knowledge, or at least refreshed our memory. Our democracy depends on the rule of law. True, laws have been used to maintain criminal social relationships, but they can also be used to promote justice and to protect the rights of children to a viable future.

Choose your Past, Choose your Future

Dec 2024

Remember the talk about "turning the page"? Turns out, we did turn the page. We turned the page back to where we had been instead of forward to something new.

We could have turned the page to write a story of dealing with the climate crisis, instead we turned back to the story of exploiting the Earth for American prosperity.

We could have turned the page to support transgender people and families, instead we turned the page back to when everyone was either a man or a woman, or in hiding.

We could have turned the page to see how the government fulfilled its job of protecting the vulnerable, instead we turned the page back to where the mythology of merit soothed the conscience of the privileged.

We could have turned the page forward where we would have had a female president, instead we turned the page backwards and ended up with a misogynist.

And so on and so on. You can add your own page turners.

It's a mistake to assume that "turning the page" would have allowed us to read a different book. It's the same book that began with enslaving laborers, occupying America, and dominating the vulnerable. Turning the page back didn't bring these stories to mind. Just the opposite, it reinforces our national amnesia.

The politics of joy may not have been sufficient, but joy could have helped us move from denial to recognition of our whole story. The problem is that we have now chosen a past without joy and with only faint hope for the future. Next time, it will be different.

STEP

16

Dissolve the Climate of Fear

The Coronavirus Exposure of Social Insecurity

Mar 2020

It would be a shame to ignore what we can learn from the coronavirus about the relationship between individual and social health. Perhaps the first lesson is that the very idea of "social health" is not in our vocabulary. We use the notion of "social security" without any problem, so it would seem that we could have a notion of "social insecurity," and wouldn't the coronavirus be a prime example of such insecurity?

The coronavirus is certainly a public health problem. No doubt about that. Without a social analysis of the epidemic, however, we ignore that the problem affects vulnerable social groups more than others. In fact, people do use social categories, such as age and health conditions, to develop a public health response to the epidemic.

This virus could help us learn something Bernie Sanders has been trying to tell us. There are 44 million people who are uninsured and almost as many have inadequate health insurance. It's a mistake to think of these people only as individuals. They are also members of social worlds that our social/economic system has created. Their vulnerability is not a "private" problem, but a "public problem," because it is a "social condition."

You do not have to be a "social democrat" to recognize the reality

151

of "social systems" and to think and talk about "social health." You do have to recognize that we are not all in the same boat. Some of us are doing quite well. Others are extremely vulnerable. A social perspective makes this quite clear.

What Happens When Fear Encounters Justice?

Sept 2020

Franklin Roosevelt famously said, "The only thing to fear is fear itself." That was in 1933, at the depth of the Great Depression, and he could assume that he was speaking for most Americans. The fears were shared. That's no longer the case.

Many are afraid that Trump will win or not leave office if Biden wins. Fewer are afraid that Trump will lose. Robert Reich's recent "This is terrifying" email exposes a significant shift from Obama's climate of hope to Trump's climate of fear.

Many fear that Trump is out of control. Trump has gotten away with violating our sense of decency and democracy so many times that one has to wonder if losing the vote will stop him. On the other hand, who is afraid of Biden? How could such a nice guy be a threat?

It's not Biden that Trump's people are afraid of. I think they are afraid that if they lose Trump, their enemies will destroy their way of life—the American way according to them. Trump did not create these fears. The fears are actually part and parcel of the "American way" itself, which has now, once again, been exposed as not what it's made out to be.

I think it's fair to say the fear of Trump's people is the fear of exposure; exposure of our nation's violations of humanity, of its devastation of the Earth, and its false narratives. Most of us who belong to privileged groups probably share this fear to some degree, but it has not frozen us. We will deal with it when we have to. There are others, however, who appear frozen in fear.

What do Trump's people fear? Anyone can make up their own list. Here are three that would be on mine.

(1) They fear multiculturalism. Multiculturalism assumes a shared humanity. It assumes that culture does not determine human dignity. It's not that all cultures are the same, but the differences are not essential. What is essential is our humanity.

(2) There is a second fear that has a long history: the fear of evolution, which was showcased in the Scopes trial in 1925. This fear not only prevents Trump's people from requiring him to address the climate crisis, but it also allows Trump's dismissal of science. One must be frozen in fear to tolerate the exposure of supporting policies that have resulted in the deaths of thousands.

(3) A third fear that maintains the climate of fear today is the fear of vulnerability. It's behind the bravado of claiming that our nation is the strongest, the best, and the most innovative. Even Biden joins in protecting us from our vulnerabilities with his rhetoric of "possibilities." In a world of winners and losers, there is no place for the acceptance of vulnerability, even mutual vulnerability, which is actually one of the few avenues to escape a climate of fear.

In terms of social climate, the climate of fear, at least in our present circumstances, has no greater enemy than a climate of justice. Trump's recent rejection of restorative justice programs in our public schools is the tip of the iceberg—the tip of a fear that the call for justice exposes as wrongheaded.

Fear by itself is neither good nor bad. It's about what is feared and why, and about what it does to the fearful. If one is full of fear, there is not much room for anything else. The opposite of fear is not courage but rather confidence: confidence that what one is protecting is worthwhile. If it doesn't measure up to the criteria of justice, I doubt if it is.

Dignity, and the Climate of Fear

June 2022

If we start with my basic premise that our colonial beginnings created a climate of injustice that has never been adequately corrected, then our conversation about gun violence would need to consider the current social climate of injustice. What difference does it make that our social climate is not a climate of justice?

In a climate of justice, we would not be afraid of each other. We may still feel uneasy with strangers, but we would not fear for our lives. In a climate of injustice, on the other hand, fear is pervasive.

Fear does seem almost universal. It's a basic human emotion. It could be that we humans are like horses, deer, and gazelles; we are fear-based animals. In my book's chapter on the civic, I refer to the work of anthropologists Donna Hart and Robert Sussman who discovered that our earliest ancestors were gatherers and scavengers, not aggressive hunters. They spent much of their energy protecting themselves from predators, such as saber-tooth tigers and pythons. If this is true, then much of our aggression may be based on the well-known premise that the best defense is a strong offense.

It's a bit more complicated. I believe that our desire for connection with others ultimately drives us, not fear. That's what I learned from attachment theory. Many of us have been lucky to live in relationships with others, and we know how fundamental these relationships are for our well-being. Some of us have not been so lucky.

A recent article on young men and guns in the *New York Times* provided research on the scary period for boys as they transition from family relationships to other social relationships (6/2/2022). When you think of their insecurity occurring in a climate of injustice, fear may well be in the driver's seat.

Wole Soyinka, the Nigerian recipient of the Noble Prize in Literature, writes in his book *Climate of Fear* that fear is a threat to a person's dignity.

> A notable aspect of all pervasive fear is that it induces a degree of loss of self-apprehension: a part of oneself has been appropriated, a level of consciousness, and this may even lead to a reduction in one's self-esteem: in short, a loss of inner dignity (p. 8).

Soyinka is not writing about mass shootings in the US, but his reflections seem to add to the ideas developed here: a climate of injustice threatens our dignity, and a climate of justice honors and protects it.

For too many today, owning a gun has become a part of their dignity, which is nothing less than a bastardization of dignity. Instead of recognizing one's dignity in reciprocal relationships with others, which would enable us to create a climate of justice, shooters stake their dignity on the power of the gun, which strengthens the climate of injustice.

This is a sticky wicket. The mixture of guns, fear, and injustices propels one to a stance that's just the opposite of what would allow the creation of a climate of justice: a stance of humility and generosity. Even the deaths of shoppers and children do not seem to break through the pride of the tyrant.

What might help is the realization that behind the climate of fear exists the legacy of injustice that has never been corrected. I doubt that we will make much progress in gun safety until we begin to dissipate the climate of fear by creating a climate of justice based on human dignity.

Acknowledge Limitations

Limiting American Prosperity

Apr 2020

If there is one thing we must learn from this epidemic, it's how to accept limits. This is not the land of "unlimited possibilities." We cannot be whatever we want to be. We should stay indoors until we learn to accept limits. If we don't, we will destroy our future on this one planet.

Even with such pleas, in all probability, we will ignore the fact of limits as we return to "normal." That may seem impossible in light of the epidemic's overwhelming disruption of our everyday lives. The problem, however, is that the epidemic has only changed the present—our current social and economic conditions—and it's not the present that shapes the future: it's the past: a past of injustice at the core of our social structures.

You may ask about the source of the inspiration of the medical caregivers, and the millions of others who have put their lives at risk to do their job of serving us. Yes, their courage and care do support and, in some instances, have created a microclimate of justice. In a climate of justice, caring for the vulnerable would be as reasonable as not providing health care in a climate of injustice.

These temporary episodes of hope, however, will have little chance of changing the legacy of injustice that is now pushing us toward a future we do not want. The momentum of the past largely controls our future. From the white compromises that allowed slavery and the Jim Crow regime, to the genocide of Indigenous peoples, to the imperialist domination of Asia, we have been carried by what I call the "tailwinds of American Prosperity," which assumes, among other things, a world of unlimited possibilities (for most white people).

To change this trajectory, we have to deflate the momentum of our history. Perhaps we can do this by listening to those who have tried to limit American advancement and then tell a new story that includes our failure to allow others to limit us. If we can tell such a story, we will not only have changed the past but the future as well.

We actually have lots of resources to re-imagine our past, including Pekka Hamalainen's book *Lakota America: A New History of Indigenous Power*. Hamalainen presents the Lakota as a Sioux empire that stopped, for a short period, the Western expansion of the federal government.

The Sioux empire of 2 to 3 thousand warriors defeated the US forces at Little Big Horn. In retaliation, the US massed their larger forces and defeated the Sioux, and then, when the Sioux tried to reclaim their dignity through the ceremony of the Ghost Dance, our military committed the Wounded Knee massacre in 1890. Hamalainen's book gives us much more than just a description of these wars. He provides us a story of a people who fought to save their territory and families— to limit American expansion. Their failure and our victory prevented us from experiencing the limits of American imperialism.

One may think that we have learned about limits elsewhere— from Vietnam, Iraq, or Afghanistan—but it doesn't look like it. Even Biden speaks as though we can be anything we want to be. The scholar Roxanne Dunbar-Ortiz may be right that the Indian Wars have served as the "template for the United States in the World" (*The Indigenous people's History of the United States*). Why else would we have "tomahawk missiles" and "Apache helicopters"? Why else engage in the killing of civilians as a war strategy? Why else refer to war zones as "Indian territory"?

There were treaties made between the American and Sioux empires, to use Hamalainen's terminology. The treaties represent a moment of coexistence, of the acceptance of limits. The expansion of American prosperity, however, led to the violation of these treaties and a reiteration of the story of American exceptionalism.

The ideology of exceptionalism has always been a threat to other peoples, and now it has become a threat to the Earth itself. Could it be that those who are among the most vulnerable today—Indigenous Americans—are the ones who could teach us about limits?

The American Tragedy

May 2021

There are different kinds of tragedy, but the American one follows a rather typical pattern. Unknown or denied past events cause one's downfall without regard to good intentions or optimistic forecasts. You can hear this in President Biden's rhetoric of "This is the United States," or "There is nothing we cannot do when we do it together." It's true that we have reached the moon, but it's also true that we nearly lost our democracy, not due to a lack of optimism, but due to a lack of historical consciousness.

I understand that Trump and Biden are as distinct as a horse and a donkey, but at times, they both resemble a mule more than one might anticipate. "Make America first" is not that different from "make America great again. "Jobs, jobs, jobs" is not that different from Trump's policies that provided jobs to more minorities than ever before.

On the other hand, Biden's cabinet exists in a totally different world than Trump's. What is not yet clear is how these two worlds will interact. One option is for Biden's world to simply expand. "Success will be its own reward." The other option is to engage in a tangle—a fight—to save our democracy. Biden seems to have taken the first option. Economic success will make dealing with voter suppression unnecessary. "America is a winner; we just need to win for all."

The character flaw behind tragedy, of course, is hubris, or for us, white arrogance. I would not accuse President Biden of arrogance, but his rhetoric belongs to an American history in which it is endemic.

Biden's Mistake

May 2021

Ok, I'm not sure. Biden is certainly better than Trump. Still, it seems like President Biden has not made the voting rights bills his top priority.

While he has twice invited Republicans to the White House to get their cooperation in passing his infrastructure bill, I have not heard about him inviting Republicans once to help pass the Senate bill on voting rights. If he thinks that repairing our infrastructure will save our democracy, I think he's making a mistake.

We are living in the wake of the January 6 insurrection, and the Republicans certainly know that this crisis is an opportunity to nail down their minority. There are well over 300 bills in different states to limit access to voting. Even major corporations, as well as professional sports, can see the danger. If we don't stop voter suppression, the Republicans are very likely to take over the House in 2022. It doesn't really make much difference if they drive to Washington on a new highway in an electric car.

It's not only that Biden wants to build back better, but better than any other nation. Where is the humility of someone who owes not only his nomination but also his election to people of color? If we want to be the world's leader in something, what about being the world's leader in paying reparations to those who have suffered from American imperialism?

We do have economic problems, but the fundamental problems we face cannot be solved with economic solutions. My view is that there is a social climate of injustice that continues to keep us from creating a sustainable future. If that is true, then trying to create such a future without changing the social climate to a climate of justice is a mistake. It may be more than a mistake; it could be the death of our democracy.

Pie in the Sky, Mud in Your Eye

May 2021

You're walking down the street, looking at the sky and "oops" there is mud in your eye. Why? Because you were not paying attention. The sky is full, of course, but you have to watch your step.

Let's load up the voting rights bill with campaign reforms. Oops, mud in your eye.

Let's get our troops out of Afghanistan. Oops, mud in your eye.

Let's get rid of Liz Chaney. Oops, mud in your eye.

I know what you are feeling. Oops, mud in your eye.

When we work together, there's nothing we cannot do. Oops mud in your eye.

Let's ignore Trump's lies. Oops, mud in your eye.

Look here: We're the United States of America. Oops, mud in your eye.

Don't criticize Biden, just remember he's better than Trump. Oops, mud in your eye

It's not that easy, especially if you believe in American exceptionalism or if you are plagued with social amnesia. If there ever was a time when we need to know where we have been and to watch where we are going, it's now.

Listening to Reinhold Niebuhr

Apr 2022

Reinhold Niebuhr was a leading theological ethicist in the middle of the 20th century. Barack Obama called Niebuhr his favorite philosopher. In an interview in 2007, President Obama said about Niebuhr's ideas:

> The compelling idea is that there's serious evil in the world, and hardship and pain. And we should be humble and modest in our belief we can eliminate these things. But we shouldn't use that as an excuse for cynicism and inaction. I take away. . . the sense we have to make those efforts knowing they are hard and not swinging from naive idealism to better realism.

Niebuhr wrote *Moral Man and Immoral Society* after his experiences with the KKK and white supremacy early in his career as a pastor in Detroit, Michigan. I assume that these experiences were part of the background of his "moral man and immoral society" formulation. Racial pride, in other words, was best understood as a group identity.

Niebuhr applied a similar perspective toward nations, not only toward our adversaries but also toward ourselves. National pride can be just as dangerous for us as for others. Once we have decided that we are the good guys and Putin is evil, I think Niebuhr would roll his eyes. Niebuhr wrote in *The Children of Light and the Children of Darkness*:

> The fact that the will-to-power inevitably justifies itself in terms of the morally more acceptable will to realize man's true nature means that the egoistic corruption of universal ideas is a much more persistent fact in human conduct than any moralistic creed is inclined to admit.

As we now "weaken" Russia on the backs of Ukrainian combatants and civilians, the danger grows that we lose awareness of the complexity of our national identity.

Learn from Differences

Good Friday Reflections During the Epidemic

April 2020

When I think as a Christian theologian, which is not that often, I often ask myself where is Jesus Christ today? To answer this question, I think one has to engage in Biblical scholarship, as I did some years ago.

So, Jesus was a Jew. He spoke Aramaic. Some scholars see evidence that he belonged to the Zealots, which was a group fighting against Roman occupation, which I tend to agree with. In any case, his identity is bound up with his execution on the cross.

As I understand it, his community was rather dumfounded. We really don't know what would happen next, because the story was written on this side of whatever happened in an attempt to make sense of it all. His community decided or maybe acknowledged that he was the Messiah. Other Jews disagreed. The Jewish tent, so to speak, was big enough for both views. To acknowledge that this person who had died on the cross was the Messiah went against a lot of assumptions. The writings about the suffering servant in Second Isaac provided some support. The larger Jewish community in Jerusalem didn't get a chance to figure all of this out because in 70 AD the Romans destroyed the Jewish Temple and the Jewish community that followed Jesus.

Another Jesus community emerged that was gentile and spoke

Greek not Aramaic. The Christian church we know today has its roots in this community and language, which opened certain possibilities and closed others. It closed the possibility of the larger Jewish community finding a way of accepting multiple interpretations of the Messiah, and the inclusion of the Jesus story in the larger Jewish story. It opened the possibility of non-Jews learning about the hope of the coming Messiah. In Greek, of course, instead of speaking of Jesus as the Messiah the talk was about Jesus Christ (Christ is the Greek word that was used to mean the Messiah).

The gentile church, lacking the Jewish context, engaged in extensive speculation about the meaning of the cross. Church leaders had conferences to work out their various theories and finally came up with a trinitarian formula of Father, Son, and Spirit to make connections between the human and the divine. What they insisted on was that Jesus was human, and that even though the divine could be distinguished from the human, it could not be separated. Compared to the Jewish view of the suffering servant, the Greek view seems quite abstract, and it put less emphasis on the Jewish Christian's view of Jesus as a suffering servant.

So, given this analysis, where do we find Jesus Christ today? The theologian James Cone gives us a clue in his powerful book *The Cross and the Lynching Tree* (2011), which recovers the notion of Jesus as a suffering servant. Cone highlights several parallels between the Roman execution of slaves, criminals, and insurrectionists (including Jesus) and the lynching of black individuals by white men. Cone writes: "The crucifixion of Jesus by the Romans in Jerusalem and the lynching of blacks by whites in the United States are so amazingly similar that one wonders what blocks the American Christian imagination from seeing the connection" (p. 30).

It takes a while for Cone's insight to sink in. It's not the usual view. The usual view is closer to the view of the Roman emperor, Constantine, who made the Christian religion the religion of the Roman Empire. How ironic that the Roman Empire that killed Jesus later made Christianity their state religion. Empires, including our own, have been known to do this. Cone's unusual view may be closer to the truth.

When I visited the Peace and Justice Memorial in Montgomery in February, I experienced it as a sacred place. There are other sacred places and experiences. Think of the hospitals, the doctors and nurses, and the separation of loved ones. Think of how the coronavirus is ripping through our communities. How it attacks the vulnerable

And how will the privilege respond? How will we experience the suffering and death of others? Will we respond as whites did to the lynching of black people? Will we respond as the followers of Jesus when they found a meaning in his death? How will we respond to the losses of this epidemic?

Afropessimism and White masters

May 2020

We all know that people read books from their own perspective, but with Frank B. Wilderson III's book *Afropessimism*, I am fully aware of being a white reader. "Afropessimism" is doubly pessimistic: pessimistic about Afro-Americans finding space to live as human beings, and pessimistic about whites being more than masters.

What's even more dreadful is that these two pessimisms are deeply intertwined. Just as you cannot have slaves without masters, you cannot have masters without slaves. Or, to put it another way, changing from a climate of injustice to a climate of justice is impossible.

People may disagree with Wilderson's argument that "Blackness cannot be separated from slavery" (p. 317), but what catches my attention is the idea that whiteness cannot be separated from masters, if I may put it that way. White and black, in other words, are interconnected in the same way as master and slave. You cannot have one without the other. And it gets worse: Whites expanded their master self-image beyond blacks to others and even to the planet. Masters of the universe. No need for masters to wear a mask.

The master/slave relationship, as Wilderson describes it, is also violent. The capacity for violence is what makes masters into masters. There is ample evidence to support such a claim. If Wilderson's story is the only story to tell, one should be pessimistic. There is another story, however, that could allow us to continue the work toward justice: the story of civilians.

True, masters have used laws to legitimize slavery, genocide, and the destruction of the planet, but we also must recognize that laws have been used to advance the rights of children, workers, women, and disenfranchised communities. Although we still live in a climate of injustice—the legacy of master/slave relationships—we can now appeal to the rule of law to protect civilians, and not just on the battlefield.

Groups that are vulnerable and cannot protect themselves have the right to demand the enforcement of the rule of law, and if those of us who have resources to combat the flouting of the rule of law take a stand, then the continuance of injustice is not inevitable. We may even create a climate of justice that expects the establishment of reciprocal relationships.

Black Lives Matter and Thanks-taking

Nov 2020

The response to the claim "Black Lives Matter" that "all lives matter" may be a sign that the speakers are unaware of the climate of injustice in which we live. The claim highlights the fact that the climate of injustice caused by American colonialists and settlers has never been repaired. Now that Thanksgiving is over, maybe we should take a look at the idea of "thanks-taking."

Thanks for taking the land.

Thanks for taking slave labor.

Thanks for taking the forests.

Thanks for taking the gold and silver.

Thanks for taking the fossil-fuels.

Thanks for taking the resources of others.

Thanks for all we have taken.

Sounds strange until we remember that capitalism is about taking—taking and making and selling. American prosperity relies on the taking from labor and land. The people and the Earth that have been taken do not matter.

This year has been phenomenal in waking us from our deep sleep in a climate of injustice. We can be thankful for that. Will we stay awake, or snooze through the Biden administration as though we did not have to change the climate of injustice to a climate of justice?

Critical Race Theory and Coherence

July 2022

The challenge of Critical Race Theory is not so much about cancel culture but rather about deciding what we should emphasize in telling our national story.

Most stories have some coherence: the parts fit together to make some kind of whole. That doesn't mean, however, that a coherent story is a good story. The story the KKK told itself probably had as much coherence for them as the story the abolitionists told themselves. A coherent story may make sense—if you live inside the story—but it may appear as non-sense from the outside. In fact, the process of moving inside and outside of stories is about the only way you can both appreciate a story's coherence and also evaluate it. We need multiple stories, in other words, to really understand the truth of a story's coherence.

Critical Race Theory says among other things that we cannot understand America without thinking about race, not in a biological sense but in a social sense. Thinking about race relations is necessary to tell a coherent American story. We can do this. In fact, the resources are now available by walking around the National Mall.

We could begin with the Washington and Jefferson Memorials, but remember they were both enslavers. Perhaps it would be more beneficial to start at the Museum of African American History and Culture, followed by a tour of the Franklin D. Roosevelt Memorial, the Martin Luther King Jr. Memorial, and a visit to the Native American Museum. From there we could visit the various war memorials and end our walk at the Lincoln Memorial. If we could imagine the relationships among these different memorials, we might get a good idea of what American coherence feels like. We might even find ourselves yearning for a climate of justice.

Joy in a Climate of Injustice

Sept 2024

What is joy in a climate of injustice? How should we think about Kamala Harris's politics of joy? First, it represents a radical contrast to the anger, hate, and resentment that have dominated the Republican Party from the rise of the Tea Party movement to Trump's campaign, Harris's politics of joy juxtaposes the dominance of white supremacy with the freedom of every individual.

Several pro-Trump social media outlets have proposed that the Harris campaign has borrowed the politics of joy from the Nazis. One such group, the Christian group "Now the End Begins" posted the following:

> In 1933, Nazi Germany rolled out something called Kraft Durch Freude, or in English, Strength Through Joy, the idea being that your source of joy was to be given to you from your Fascist government. In 2024, Comrade Kamala wants to do the very same thing.

Most of the time, apocalyptic groups are not worth writing about, but when such groups have followers who are voters, then their twisted associations and fabrications need a response. As she says time and time again, joy is not about domination, but freedom, such as freedom to control your body, or freedom to love who you love, or freedom from gun violence.

People are also free to tell lies. They may even enjoy doing so. "Joy," it seems, can be used for every different purpose, or to put it another way, it can belong to very different contexts or social worlds. What does it mean in the context of a climate of injustice?

In a recent article in the *New York Times* entitled: "Where Joy Meets Anger: Harris and Trump Battle for Undecided Voters" (9/21/24), one person the writers interviewed said, "But what are we supposed to do, have joy for inflation? For rising rent? What am I supposed to be joyful about?" If I understand Harris's view of joy, it is not about doing something but rather about being something. Joy belongs to our humanity and our power to thrive even in an unjust world.

That's the answer I find in Tracey Michael Lewis Giggetts' book *Black Joy: Stories of Resistance, Resilience, and Restoration* (2022). She writes:

> White supremacy and our struggle against it are not the only things that binds us together as Black people. In fact, it isn't even the most interesting part of who we are. That said, the experiences of the descendants of African people (the enslaved particularly) are convoluted at best and therefore our joy is ever intertwined with our struggle; ever integrated with the trauma wielded against us. You are surely going to have to use a different lens to witness this particular brand of joy—maybe even in these essays—but I assure you that if you're willing to see it, it's willing to be seen. Black joy is both pervasive and petty that way. No game of peekaboo here, though. Just an unwillingness to contort itself in order to become some beacon

of light for the world. No, Black joy, no matter how complicated, knows its survival lies in the ability for every vessel it fills to remain free even on the inside (xxiii).

Years ago, a Black woman told me that we do not have a "common humanity," but rather a "shared humanity" This rings true once we realize that the development of our humanity occurs in some social world. I see Kamala Harris willing to share the human joy of Black people living in our racist nation, which is nothing less than a gift that we must surely need.

Engage in Ethical Analysis

The Ethics of Biden's Withdrawal from Afghanistan.

Sept 2021

President Biden's decision to withdraw from Afghanistan by September 1 came, as he said, from his very core. For him, it was the right thing to do. Why? Because he followed his "moral compass," so to speak. Most of us have some kind of moral compass that helps us make good decisions. As we know, some compasses are better than others. It all depends on what our moral compass encompasses

A good moral compass guides you toward your goal, but it also checks out your will or desire to make the journey and exposes how your decision will impact the circumstances of others. In my book *The Ethical Process* (2003), I called these the ethics of purpose, principle, and consequence. In *Learning through Disagreement* (2014), I presented the three as the activities of a visionary, a judge, and a calculator. Whatever their names, a good moral compass does not focus on one of these three at the expense of the others.

The Ethics of Purpose

It did seem to me that President Biden focused first of all on our national interest. National interest, in other words, was the goal, and the withdrawal of troops was the "means toward the end." Central to an ethics of purpose is the relationship between means and ends—acts and goals. If the end is good, then the means are justified. One might quibble about the means, but if their negative impact does not outweigh the good accomplished, the action is justified.

One could say that the withdrawal was not so much an action that furthered our national interest but one that stopped its violation. Generally, we use an ethics of purpose to justify good deeds, but in this case, we used it to stop harm—damage to our national interest. One could imagine other cases where a similar decision would be quite appropriate, depending on how we understand what's in our "national interest."

Ethics of Principle

When President Biden chose this action, he also willed a moral principle, or at least that's what an ethics of principle would assume. Instead of the good purpose justifying the right decision, in this case, the right decision depends on what kind of decision it was; that is, on whether others could make a similar decision in similar situations. So, could we always withdraw like this? No, not if it broke our promises.

From an ethics of principle perspective, it is imperative not to break promises because if you did, no one would make them with you again. The promise here, as you know, was to protect Afghans who had worked with us. This ethical approach would surely spin the needle on our moral compass.

Ethics of Consequence

Ok, decisions can be complicated. That's why we have three types of analysis instead of one. It decreases the chance of making a mistake. The third one looks at how the action impacts others and their circumstances. The withdrawal is certainly positive for our military. For Afghan civilians, especially women, it's horrible.

For the overall circumstances of the area, the withdrawal probably does not change the conditions of war. We have withdrawn our soldiers, but we have not done much to decrease the trafficking in weapons, war profiteering, or the plight of vulnerable civilians.

When our moral compass encompasses purpose, principle and consequence, the needle may take several spins before it shows us the way, and that could be a mistake. My guess is that if the decision increases the climate of injustice, it is.

An Ethical Foundation for Environmentalism

Aug 2022

Reading the books, *Settler Memory* by Kevin Bruyneel and *Braiding Sweetgrass* by Robin Wall Kimmerer has led me to reflect again on the significance of the sub-title of *A Climate of Justice*: "An Ethical Foundation for Environmentalism." The following is not a review of their books but rather reflections on different foundations for an environmental ethic. I highly recommend both books.

Bruyneel defines "settler memory" as the telling of American stories that omit the suffering of Indigenous peoples. Settler memory, in other words, is defined by the stories that settlers do not tell, especially the stories of the commandeering and genocide of Indigenous peoples.

Correcting the failure of settler memory requires that we include the legacy of our nation's disruption of Indigenous peoples as well as the enslavement of Africans is telling the story of white supremacy, which I see as the barrier to environmental sustainability. This correction could include such actions as the elimination of "Indian" mascots and names in sports and the switch from Columbus Day to Indigenous Peoples' Day, as is already happening in some communities. At a more significant level, the correction would stop the continued exploitation of land and people for profit.

I don't think Bruyneel would have much trouble agreeing with my argument that we live in a climate of injustice, but I am not sure if he would follow me to imagine empowered civilians making claims before government representatives for protection and provisions based on the rule of law. It could be, of course, that the most we can hope for is that vulnerable civilians create solidarity with each other and fight to survive in a climate of injustice. In this case, the basis for an environmental ethic would be resistance to American imperialism.

Robin Wall Kimmerer also writes about memory: the memory of ancestors. The memory of ancestors and their stories guide us to listen and respond to the "teaching of plants." Instead of an ethic of resistance, Kimmerer invites us to participate in reciprocal relationships with plants.

> One of our responsibilities as human people is to find ways to enter into reciprocity with the more than human world. We can do it through gratitude, through ceremony, through land stewardship, science, art, and in very day acts of practical reverence (p.190).

Whether we recognize such an invitation depends on our perspective. Seeing nature as a commodity, of course, prevents us from entering reciprocal relationships. Seeing nature as a gift, on the other hand, sets up the possibility of feeling gratitude for what the Earth has given us. As she says, "reciprocity is a matter of keeping the gift in motion through self-perpetuating cycles of giving and receiving (165).

I also use the ethical principle of reciprocity in *A Climate of Justice*, but not exactly as Kimmerer does. I also argue that the Earth should not be seen as merely property or a commodity, but I do not have the knowledge she has about the layers of relationships between humans and plants. Perhaps the easiest way to explore these differences is to use the four-fold interpretative framework I provide in the first part of *A Climate of Justice*: Earth, our humanity, the social, and the civic.

Kimmerer's stories show the reciprocal relationships between plants and people. I argue that the Earth should be seen as our shared habitat or home, which is not contrary to her perspective.

I also see humans as belonging to the Earth, but I do something she does not: I employ the research of neurobiology to locate human dignity in our core awareness of our purposeful existence. My guess is that Kimmerer would see this as very Western because it locates the origin of dignity in the body rather than in reciprocal relationships. At the same time, we would likely agree that the experience of our dignity occurs in social relations.

If we see our social worlds as constituted by the stories we tell, then I think we would agree on the significance of our social identity. The difference would be the stories we tell. My analysis of the American social includes the stories of the exploitation of both cheap labor and cheap land: enslaved and Indigenous peoples. Here I find myself more in alignment with Bruyneel's critique of settler memory than Kimmerer's ancestor memory.

Neither Kimmerer nor Bruyneel provide much information that aligns with the fourth element of my framework: the civic. I see the civic as the gathering of civilians who press for their rights to protection and provision from those who have the resources and the legal obligations to respond to their requests. I argue that the civic repair of injustices will create a climate of justice, which is based on reciprocal relationships of all inhabitants of the Earth.

I learned from Bruyneel that this transformation may not happen. I think I rely more on the thoughts of Martin Luther King Jr., who not only called for resistance to white supremacy but also called our government to fulfill its promises and obligations to vulnerable civilians.

Reading Kimmerer's book reminded me of my childhood on a farm in Nebraska. My ancestors did not tell me about reciprocal relationships with plants, and yet I did experience the beauty and the danger of Nebraska weather. The year a hailstorm ruined our crops, I didn't think of reciprocity. Hailstorms, as they say, fall on the just and the unjust.

It's clear to me that the "ethical principle of environmentalism" must see the Earth as a limited living system. White supremacy denies limits. Reciprocity imposes limits. I think we encounter the limits not only with the Earth but also with vulnerable civilians who have a right to protection and provisions. Environmental ethics, in other words, is not only about our relationship with the Earth but also each other.

Three Images of Our Federal Government

Aug 2023

It seems abundantly clear that we cannot adequately address the climate crisis without the appropriate government policies and regulations. Our dilemma stems from the fact that many popular images are impeding the government's ability to perform its duties effectively. If we cannot imagine the government protecting the planet, it's probably not going to happen. So, we need to check our images. There are many, of course, and here are three.

1. An alien encroaching on local sovereignty.

Following the Civil War, the Federal "Freedman's Bureau" brought needed assistance to newly freed Blacks. For some whites, those who gave assistance were seen as carpetbaggers (white Northerners) or scallywags (white Southerners) who were preventing a return to "normal" southern life.

In his book *Freedom's Dominion: A Saga of White Resistance to Federal Power (2022),* Jefferson Cowie illustrates time and again the dominance of the image of the federal government as an intruder on local and state sovereignty—the freedom to dominate others.

> Combatting the freedom to dominate in its most visceral forms, as Native Americans trying to enforce treaty rights and African Americans struggling for the freedom of political participation during Reconstruction learned, required a social contract in which the federal government worked aggressively to restrain the freedom of the dominant class. In the case of lynching, the federal government could never manage to make lynching illegal despite the introduction of literally hundreds of anti-lynching bills in the 20th century. (241).

This image, like the image of federal government as a bunch of carpetbaggers and scallywags, belongs to the legacy of the Lost Cause, which continues to influence the attitudes of many white Americans.

2. A reluctant protector of civil rights:

Because our nation started as a slave nation (4 out of the first 5 Presidents were enslavers), the movements for human rights have always been an uphill battle, and yet, things have improved. Still, the struggle continues largely within the context of our original social climate of injustice.

3. A "Criminal Enterprise"

Remember that the RICO case against Trump and his gang refers to their actions while still in office. Did they make our government a "criminal enterprise"? Well, no. Our government also upholds the rule of law, and we have laws that protect our democracy, or at least that's how it looks in this case. Still, until we recover from our original crimes against humanity, any flag waving would be not only premature but also a lie.

Ethics of Politics

Feb 2024

The people who stormed the Capital on Jan 6 have deep historical roots reaching back to the story of the Lost Cause, which emphasized that even though white Southerners had lost the war, their "cause" was more noble than that of the Federal invaders. They rose again as a backlash to the liberation movements of the 1960s. Their current themes revolve around the threats they see to their America by so called "elites," people of color, immigrants, and progressives. They believe Trump can save America as a bastion of freedom, or at least block infringements on their freedom.

You must wonder why some people seem more comfortable in a climate of injustice than in a climate of justice. It's true justice always refers to relations and assumes some bonds among individuals. Freedom, on the other hand, can be seen as non-relational, but even with this one-sided view of freedom, Trump would still have a people—a people of individuals.

The word "people" is ambiguous. One reads "We the people of the United States" at the beginning of our Constitution (even though 40% of Virginia's population was enslaved) and Abraham Lincoln concludes his Gettysburg Address, with the words: "government of the people, by the people, and for the people, shall not perish from the Earth." It seems to me that his hope has not been extinguished, but neither has it been fulfilled. We are a nation and an empire of peoples, not of a people.

Still, the principle, if not the reality of democracy is that political power resides in the people. "Power to the People." The Latin American philosopher, Enrique Dussel, has given us a way to talk about people and power. Dussel died in November last year at the age of 88. For decades, he had been a leading Latin American philosopher. Born in Argentina, he escaped to Mexico during the Argentinian dictatorship. He is one of the founders of the philosophy of liberation and has written many books and articles, including *The Ethics of Liberation*.

Political power, as Dussel defines it, has two dimensions. The first is people power, which he calls, *potentia,* the power that arises from communal consensus. The actualization of this communal power depends on its delegation or institutionalizing, which Dussel calls *potestas* power, the power of the representative. Here it gets tricky. Representatives can either remain obedient to the community—their power source—or take the communal power for themselves. Instead of serving the people, they dominate them.

> The fundamental link between *potestas* (the power that must be exercised through delegation), and *potentia* (the power of the *people* itself) is broken, and the

former is thereby absolutized, claiming itself as a self-reflective and self-referential foundation.

In such cases, the power relationship has been inverted. Instead of the delegate following the people, the people follow the delegate. Doesn't this fit Trump and his people to a tee? As Trump has repeatedly said, he could stand in the middle of Fifth Avenue and shoot somebody and not lose any voters. Once a people's power has been stolen from them (or given to him), it follows that Trump's enemies become their enemies, and democracy loses its validity. They have put their faith in Trump rather than in democratic institutions.

As we hinted earlier, not all "people" are the same, and Trump's people are certainly not what Dussel had in mind when writing his ethics and politics of liberation. Dussel's first fact, which he takes from neurobiology, is that humans will to live and to live in a community. Therefore, human communities will get those things they need to survive. From this fact, Dussel proposes a "material ethics." Instead of freedom or recognition, he proposes that we begin our thinking with human needs—the people's material conditions. Dussel writes:

> The clearest and most definitive point of departure for the entire framework of criticism that I have developed is the relationship produced between the negation of the corporality, the bodily reality (*Leiblichkeit*) reflected in the suffering of the victims, of all those dominated (as workers, Indigenous people. African slaves, or exploited Asians in the colonized world; as the bodily reality of women, of those who are not white, of the few generations who will suffer the effects of ecological destruction: all the elderly without a place in a consumer society, children abandoned in the streets, all those excluded because they are foreigners, immigrants, or refugees, etc.), and the process by which the victims become conscious of this negation. (*Ethics of Liberation*, p. 215).

For Dussel, the aim of philosophy, as Karl Marx said, is not just to understand the world but to change it. To negate the negations of the lives of victims, such as negating the negative of hunger by providing access to food, gives them the capacity (the power) to change the world.

Does that sound like Trump's people? Are their material conditions like the poor, the homeless, the hungry, or the refugee? If not, are they helping material victims gain resources to liberate themselves? If not, are they blocking any advancement toward a climate of justice?

Trump's people have always been part of our history. I don't know if they will learn that there are causes—from multicultural education to environmental protection—that they could help us win. My guess is that movements toward a climate of justice must happen without them.

Ethics of the 14th Amendment

June 2024

One of the principles of ethics is "just because it's legal, doesn't make it right." In fact, one could make a long list of laws that allowed the wrongful treatment of others. Still, one cannot say for sure that the Supreme Court would do the right thing by not upholding the law of the 14th Amendment. It depends on our ethical analysis.

In the past, the focus has been mostly on the 14th Amendment's principles of due process and equal protection. Now, it's Section 3, which one could see as an attempt to protect the necessary context for equal justice. It states that anyone who has taken an oath to support the Constitution and then engages in an insurrection shall not be allowed to hold public office again.

The legal case seems clear especially for a Supreme Court dominated by justices who use an originalist interpretation of the Constitution and have supported the sovereignty of states over the federal government.

Some Justices, possibly even the majority, may desire to renounce their originalist beliefs and permit Trump to run in all 50 states. If they don't follow the law, however, how will they justify their decision? What ethical principles will they use? A careful ethical analysis should consider at least three things: the purpose of the Court, the logical consistency of its decision, and the decision's probable consequences (see my *The Ethical Process*).

I would say that the Court's purpose is to protect the legitimacy of our democracy. If keeping one's public oath is central to democratic legitimacy, then the Court should either allow states to disqualify Trump or decide to do it themselves. The court could also act with consistency in all such cases. Can you imagine a common practice of public officials making oaths and then violating them? So, it seems that an ethics of purpose and principle would favor disqualifying Trump.

The assessment of consequences is more complex. When a cult leader is dethroned, what will the followers do? If he is not, what will the rest of us do? When an ethics of purpose and an ethics of principle support disqualifying Trump, it is usually unwise to let an ethics of consequence change the decision. One might hope that the Supreme Court makes such an assessment, but that would mean that the majority do not belong to the cult.

20

Stand with Others for Social Justice

The Dangers of Compromise

Aug 2020

If you were visiting from almost anywhere, you would want to know why we have over 154,000 coronaviruses deaths.

One answer is the lack of leadership. Not just Trump, but also some governors and mayors, who place their personal ambition ahead of the lives of others. The more fundamental question, however, is not why these elected officials do not protect their constituents, but rather why do we let them get away with it?

I think the answer is that we would rather compromise than destroy. We allow terrible things because stopping them would, we fear, destroy our institutions, social order and American prosperity. This is an old pattern, beginning with the Compromise of 1788 when the Northern and Southern states agreed to count enslaved people as $3/5^{th}$ of a person so the slave states would join the Union.

After the period of Reconstruction, the "white compromise" of 1877 allowed whites to "redeem" the South and to control the North until the 1960s. The pattern was then suspended but not replaced, and it appears to have gained control again with Trump in the White House.

Trump's regime has committed crimes against humanity. How else can one interpret our government's treatment of families at our southern border? His mishandling of the pandemic has resulted in thousands of deaths. Still, as we come closer to the national election, we treat him as though he were a legitimate president. As Nancy Pelosi has suggested, we don't need to respect the person, but we should respect the office. So, the political parties, in spite of the pandemic, have scheduled presidential debates as though things were quite ordinary.

There are those, in Portland and elsewhere, who have rejected this pattern of compromise. "If our compromises have prevented us from standing up for the truth, then stop compromising." The fact is that the truth itself is complicated, and we usually get to more of the whole truth through compromise than through single-mindedness. Still, there are compromises that promote justice as well as compromises that promote injustice. We need to know the difference.

In the 2000 election, Al Gore compromised by agreeing not to insist on a recount of the vote in Florida because it would have disrupted the electoral process. So, we got George Bush, the invasion of Iraq, and a war that continues. Yes, it's complicated, but avoiding the complexity makes for unjust compromises.

When compromises cover up complexities, they are probably mistakes. When complexities are analyzed and discussed, then some compromise may result. It's an imperfect world. Nothing is more complicated than the upcoming election. We should not cover up the truth for the sake of maintaining the appearance of civility.

I could see the Democratic Party refusing to have television debates with Trump because he does not deserve the recognition that would entail. Such a stance might also honor the men and women who would still be alive if he had done his job.

71 Million and National Unity

Nov 2020

We elected Joe Biden and Kamala Harris. That's majority rule! Yet, seventy-one million of us voted for a racist predator who has committed crimes against humanity. That's phenomenal!

We shouldn't assume that 71 million racist predators, who have committed such evil acts as putting children in cages or allowing thousands to die from the coronavirus, exist among us, simply because they voted for someone who has done so. Still, it's hard to exaggerate the importance of making the right decision in responding to the calls for national unity.

What we know for sure is that Trump did not create their values and attitudes. They are part and parcel of American history, from the reluctance of the slave states to join the Union, to the Lost Cause mythology developed after the Civil War to the popular resentment toward the "elites" today. In most of our history, we have contained this "dis-unity" through compromises: the compromises of 1788, 1820, 1850, and the compromise of 1877, which allowed white supremacists to take over the South and to segregate and discriminate in the North until the 1960's. These compromises "fixed" the national "dis-unity" among whites at the expense of everyone else.

I don't think another "white compromise" is possible. White rule is over. Joe Biden owes his election to African Americans. We now have a significant "unity' among whites and people of color that could move us toward a climate of justice. The temptation is to make compromises with the "Trump whites" at the expense of others. That is what we have done before. If we want to chart a new course, we cannot do it again.

Our Choice: Unity or Justice

Jan 2021

The essential contribution of African Americans in the election of Joe Biden and in the election of Raphael Warnock and Jon Ossoff (giving Democrats control of the Senate), plus Trump's insurrection, gives us the opportunity to choose between unity and justice. This is not the first time our nation has faced such a choice. It may be the first time we choose justice.

Choosing unity rather than justice may not represent the "soul" of America, but it certainly describes our habitual behavior as a nation. We see it in the compromises of 1788, 1820, 1850, and the "white" compromise of 1877 that lasted until the 1960s. The unity was always among conflicting white groups, never between whites and people of color.

Who can be against the "healing" of our divisions? Let's just make sure that we choose the right divisions. We need to choose those divisions that prevent us from creating a sustainable future. The fact is that attempts to heal the divisions among white people will not change the climate of injustice that has shaped our choices from colonial times to today.

The current division among whites has its origin with the Southern white response to losing the Civil War. Out of their experience of being defeated by the North, they developed the ideology of the Lost Cause, which proclaimed that their "cause" was more just and righteous than the North's.

This injury to their white pride, as I understand it, became a sign of their sacrifice for white supremacy. Their "noble suffering," in other words, stiffened their self-righteousness. The "losers" believed they were superior to the "winners." Just like today, many Republicans believe they are more righteous and even more American than the Democrats.

Attempts to unify these white differences have little chance of dealing with the issue that prevents us from moving from a climate of injustice to a climate of justice: the issue of white arrogance. Just like in past national compromises, whites will again join together in advancing American prosperity at the expense of people and the planet.

This is a historical moment. If we see it as the election when African Americans and other people of color secured the future of our democracy, then we might let them help us move toward a climate of justice. Or, if we see it as the election that revealed the deep antagonism between whites, then I suspect we will repeat a pattern that is as old as our nation.

The Voice of Social Justice

Jan 2021

As I approached the Martin Luther King Jr. Memorial in the month before the pandemic, I heard a recording of Dr. King's voice, a voice that for me sounds like social justice. I first heard Dr. King's voice in 1965 in Montgomery, Alabama. I had been in Montgomery for a week with a few other white students. We were asked to come to Montgomery's black community to make KKK attacks less likely. When the marchers from Selma arrived at Montgomery, we joined them in a march through the city to the state capital, where Dr. King spoke. I was not close to the stage, but I was there.

I heard Dr. King a second time in a small church in Chicago in 1967. I was spending the summer working for the Chicago City Missionary Society with Black teenagers from the south side of Chicago. On a hot evening, in a crowded church, I could hear his voice as I stood just inside the sanctuary.

The last time I heard Martin Luther King's voice was at Riverside Church in New York, when he came out against the Vietnam War. This time, I sat in a pew not far from the pulpit, and I felt in the presence of the voice of social justice. He addressed the rights and perils not only of the civilians of the United States but also of the civilians of Vietnam.

In the terminology of my current thinking, he exposed the climate of injustice and called for a climate of justice.

His voice, like the voice of Malcolm X, Bobby Kennedy, Fred Hampton, and others, was silenced with a gun. The fact is that the voices of social justice are always at the mercy of the gun.

Index

Symbols

14th Amendment 24, 50, 54, 70, 179

A

acceptance of limits 158
Afghanistan 170
Afropessimism 164
Agriculture Fairness Alliance 132
American context 5
American Dream. 126
American Empire 146
American exceptionalism 158, 160
American imperialism 173
American Prosperity xii, 8, 9, 29, 42, 72, 81, 89, 146, 157, 158, 166, 181, 185
America's soul 68
Anthony, Carl 105
anti-racism programs 28
Aristotle 15, 125
Athanasiou, Tom 41
Atlantic commerce 7, 42, 48, 119
Attachment theory 154

B

Barrett, Amy Coney 49, 110
Battle of the Little Big Horn 120
Bellah, Robert 30

Berry, Wendell 16
Blackhawk, Maggie 76
Black Lives Matter 4, 14, 60, 97, 133, 165
Bruyneel. Kevin 172
Burke, Kenneth 103

C

capitalism 29, 77, 124, 145, 166
Catholic originalists 54
changing course 17, 146
Chemerinsky, Erwin 54
Christian church 163
Christian imagination 14, 15, 16, 163
Christianity 123
Christian nationalism 32, 71
Christian nationalists 56, 73
Christian Zionism 31
Circle of Justice 134
citizenship 25
civic conscience 25
civic context 23, 87
civic economy 129
civic imagination, 14, 15
civic obligations 3
civic realm 13, 16, 18, 37, 57
civic solemnity 55, 56
civic space 3, 14, 24

civic sphere 15, 28, 33, 37, 59, 77, 97, 108, 126
civil government 62
Civilian Conservation Corps 61
Civilian Review Board 3, 14, 27, 59, 135
civil religion 30, 31
Civil Rights 176
civil rights movement 88
Civil War 54, 58, 94, 95, 144, 184
climate crisis 1, 41, 68, 71, 86, 134, 148, 153, 175
Coates, Ta-Nehisi 85
coherence, principle of 74
coherent story 166
combatants and civilians 88
Cone, James 163
confederate monuments 94
constitutional democracy 53
contextual awareness 103
contextual differences 108
contextual thinking 101, 102
cooperation 12, 137, 140, 159
Cooper-White. Pamela 71
COP27 meeting 9
coronavirus 3, 43, 44, 89, 92, 130, 133, 147, 151, 164, 181
corporate leaders 12
corporations 128, 129
Cowie, Jefferson 175
create money 133
crimes against humanity 4, 15, 42, 65, 95, 109, 110, 182
Crist, Meehan 145
Critical Race Theory 166

D

Damasio, Antonio 38, 100

Darling, Linda 134
D.E.I 97
DiAngelo, Robin 119
dignity, inherent 35
dignity, origin of 174
Douglas, Kelly Brown 69
Dunbar-Ortiz, Roxanne 61, 124, 157
Dussel, Enrique 177

E

Earth's integrity 44, 45
economy. purpose 26
enslavement 8
environmental justice 41, 42, 105
Equal protection 50
Equal Protection Clause 54
equal protection under the law 50
essential workers 133, 139
ethical analysis 179, 180
European ancestors xii
European immigrants 74

F

fascists 87
fear of vulnerability 153
Floyd George 133
Foner, Eric 138
Frankl, Victor 99
freedom to leave 83
French, David 97
Fuller, Buckminster 82

G

Geneva Conventions to protect civilians 13, 58
Giggellt, Tracey Michael Lewis 168
global environment 1

government funding 142
Great Depression 89

H

Haitian revolution 64
Hamalainen, Pekka 157
Hart, Donna 154
Heschel, Abraham J. 63
human dignity 38, 39, 93, 153, 155
human nature 42

I

Indigenous Americans 158
Indigenous people 6, 8, 74, 157
Indigenous Peoples' Day 96, 172
individualism 42, 106, 119, 123
International Humanitarian
    Law 13
interpretative theory 55

J

Jennings,Willie James 14
Jeremiah 63, 64
Julianna v United States 148

K

killing of civilians 61, 157
Kimmerer, Robin Wall 46, 72, 172
King, Martin Luther Jr 7, 38, 70,
    105, 108, 142, 174, 185
Kurzweil, Ray 99

L

language of domination 99
language of war 88
Lewis, John 29
libertarianism 119

limits 42, 81, 156
Lost Cause 18, 94, 108, 183, 184
lynching 175

M

master/slave relationship 164
Meacham, Jon 6, 69
meat processing plants 93, 130,
    131, 132
Moore, Michael 41
moral compass 170
multicultural context 110
Multi-culturalism 153
Museum for African American
    History and Culture 109

N

National Mall 109, 167
National Public Radio 142
national unity 183
Native Americans 64, 70, 74, 75,
    112, 175
natural environment 62, 129
Nguyen, Viet Thanh 103
Nichols, Tyre 105
Niebuhr, Reinhold 161

O

O'Gieblyn, Maghan 99
originalist 49, 50

P

pandemic 102, 133, 145, 182
Peace and Justice Memorial 164
Pence, Mike 31
Perry, Samuel 71
political climate 24
Powers, Richard 43

privileged groups 152
promissory note 7, 70
protection of civilians 48, 58, 65
public as government 142
public discourse 137
public health 60, 91, 92, 93,
    94, 151
public realm 17, 18, 27, 28, 60, 93

R

Raheb, Mitri 31
reciprocity 3, 9, 12, 100, 137,
    173, 174
Reconstruction 144, 181
Reich, Rob 84
repair of social relations 8, 118
reparations 12, 79, 82, 83, 84, 86,
    87, 159
Republican Party 142
resentment 94
Ricoeur, Paul 108
rights of civilians 28, 59, 61
Roosevelt, Franklin 152
rule of law 13, 30, 48, 53, 58, 59,
    60, 62, 76, 121, 124, 126,
    140, 149, 150, 165, 176

S

Sally Hemings 6, 96
Sanders, Bernie 151
separation of church and state
    37, 39
sharecropping 138, 139
shared humanity 29, 37, 39, 81, 82,
    97, 98, 122, 123, 153
sharing money 141
sharing relationships 137
Siedentop, Larry 123

Siegel, Daniel 100
Sioux empire 157
slave labor camps 69
social context 1, 2, 28, 70, 72, 86
social diversity 97
social habits 147
social insecurity 151
social microclimates 72
social perspective 152
social relations 3, 79, 80, 81
social systems 9, 11, 81, 147, 152
social worlds 13, 16, 17, 35, 42, 61,
    69, 71, 81, 84, 92, 93, 95,
    101, 107, 118, 125, 151, 174
solemn occasions 56, 102
Southern Tenant Farmers
    Union 139
Soyinak, Wole 154
Speth, Gus 148
Supreme Court 30, 38, 49, 53, 54,
    112, 128, 179, 180
Sussman, Robert 154
sustainable future 14
systems of provision 130

T

The Burghers of Calais 29
theory of interpretation 32
theory of originalism 54, 110
Thomas Jefferson 96
Treaty of 1763 64
true believers 108
Trump followers 11, 33, 36, 56,
    77, 127
Trump's people 152, 178, 179

U

UAW strike 11

undocumented workers 131
unjust compromises 182
unsustainable future 12

V

voter suppression 159
vulnerable civilians 94, 172,
   173, 174

W

We the People 111
white compromises 67, 70, 157
Whitehead, Andrew 71
white male arrogance 81
white male social world 101
white social world 110, 118,
   119, 125
white supremacy 2, 4, 15, 16, 27,
   74, 82, 88, 95, 108, 110, 111,
   118, 124, 126, 127, 147, 161,
   172, 174, 184
Wilderson, Frank B. 164
Wiley, Kehinde 39
Wolin, Sheldon 25
World Cup 10
world of unlimited possibilities 157
Wounded Knee 157
Wounded Knee Massacre 120
Wright, George C. 17

About the Author

Marvin Brown's work has been largely shaped by his effort to integrate his academic background in theology and philosophy with a long-term career of teaching and writing in the area of social and business ethics.

Soon after Marvin finished his doctorate in theology and rhetoric at Graduate Theological Union in 1978, he began teaching social ethics at the University of San Francisco. Drawing on what he learned from his students and mentors, Brown published Working Ethics (Jossey-Bass), in 1990, followed in 1993 by The Ethical Process (Prentice-Hall).

During the 1990s, Brown worked as an ethics and diversity consultant for such organizations as Levi Strauss and Company. In the following decades, he was invited to give lectures and workshops in Germany, Poland, Argentine, Venezuela, Norway, Canada, and China.

Brown's contact with colleagues and other authors fostered the writing of Corporate Integrity (Cambridge University Press) in 2005, Civilizing the Economy (Cambridge University Press) in 2010, and A Climate of Justice (Springer) in 2022. His books, and papers, have been translated into Spanish, Portuguese, German, Italian, Korean, and Chinese. In 2020, Brown started the blog Climate of Justice Project, which serves as a platform for writing about the possibilities for a social climate of justice, as a necessary condition for the survival of our planet.

Marvin has received an Alumni Achievement Award from Nebraska Wesleyan University and a Lifetime Service Award from the Philosophy Department at the University of San Francisco

Printed in the United States
by Baker & Taylor Publisher Services